WALKING IN
NORTHUMBERLAND

About the Author

Vivienne is an award-winning freelance writer and photographer specialising in travel and the outdoors. A journalist since 1990, she abandoned the constraints of a desk job on regional newspapers in 2001 to go travelling. On her return to the UK, she decided to focus on the activities she loves the most – hill walking, writing, travelling and photography. Needless to say, she's never looked back!

Based in north Cumbria, she has put her intimate knowledge of northern England to good use over the years, writing more than a dozen popular walking guidebooks. She also contributes to a number of regional and national magazines, including several regular walking columns, and does copywriting for conservation and tourism bodies. Vivienne is a member of the Outdoor Writers and Photographers Guild.

Other Cicerone guides by the author
Walking in Cumbria's Eden Valley
Lake District: High Level and Fell Walks
Lake District: Low Level and Lake Walks

WALKING IN
NORTHUMBERLAND

Vivienne Crow

JUNIPER HOUSE, MURLEY MOSS,
OXENHOLME ROAD, KENDAL, CUMBRIA LA9 7RL
www.cicerone.co.uk

© Vivienne Crow 2018
First edition 2018
ISBN: 978 1 85284 900 9

Replaces the previous Cicerone guide to Northumberland by Alan Hall
ISBN: 978 1 85284 428 8
Second edition 2004
First edition 1998

Printed in China on behalf of Latitude Press
A catalogue record for this book is available from the British Library.
All photographs are by the author unless otherwise stated.

Updates to this Guide

While every effort is made by our authors to ensure the accuracy of guide-books as they go to print, changes can occur during the lifetime of an edition. Any updates that we know of for this guide will be on the Cicerone website (www.cicerone.co.uk/900/updates), so please check before planning your trip. We also advise that you check information about such things as transport, accommodation and shops locally. Even rights of way can be altered over time.

We are always grateful for information about any discrepancies between a guidebook and the facts on the ground, sent by email to updates@cicerone.co.uk or by post to Cicerone, Juniper House, Murley Moss, Oxenholme Road, Kendal LA9 7RL, United Kingdom.

Register your book: to sign up to receive free updates, special offers and GPX files where available, register your book at www.cicerone.co.uk.

Front cover: Dunstanburgh Castle (Walk 2)

CONTENTS

Route symbols on OS map extracts
(for OS legend see printed OS maps)

(🚶) start point   (🚶) finish point   (🚶) start/finish point

〜 route   ◀ route direction

Features on the overview map

—— County/Unitary boundary

—— National boundary

Urban area

National Park
eg *NORTHUMBERLAND*

Forest Park/National Forest
eg *National Forest*

Area of Outstanding Natural
Beauty/National Scenic Area
eg *Northumberland Coast*

800m
600m
400m
200m
75m
0m

Acknowledgements

The author wishes to thank the following for their help with this guide-book: Andy Chymera, Senior Public Transport Project Officer at Northumberland County Council; Alex Bell, Definitive Map Officer at Northumberland County Council; Northumberland walking guide and co-owner of Footsteps, Patrick Norris; Alex MacLennan and Richard Gilchrist, of the Forestry Commission; history enthusiast and keen walker Raymond Greenhow; Martin O'Loughlin, of Natural England; and the Northumberland Estates. A particularly big thank you to Heleyne and Jess for accompanying me on most of these walks, and for being patient models whenever the camera appeared.

Looking across to Bamburgh Castle from Lindisfarne (Walk 4)

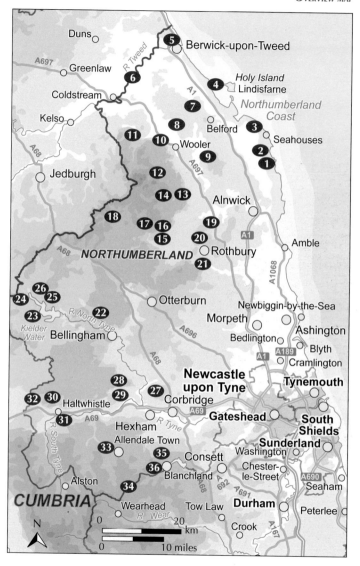

Duns

A697

Greenlaw

Coldstream

Kelso

A68

Jedburgh

5 Berwick-upon-Tweed

R Tweed

6

4 Holy Island
Lindisfarne

Northumberland
Coast

7

8 Belford

3

11 **10** Wooler Seahouses

9 **2**

1

12

14 **13**

Alnwick

18 **17** **16**

15

19

20

NORTHUMBERLAND Rothbury

21

Amble

A1

A68

A1068

26 **25**

24

23 **22** Otterburn

Kielder
Water Bellingham

R North Tyne

Newbiggin-by-the-Sea

Morpeth

Ashington

Bedlington

A189 Blyth

Cramlington

A68

A696

A1

28

29 **27**

Corbridge

**Newcastle
upon Tyne**

Tynemouth

32 **30**

Haltwhistle

31 A69

Hexham

R Tyne

A69

Gateshead

**South
Shields**

33 Allendale Town

35 Consett

36

Blanchland

Washington

Sunderland

Chester-
le-Street

A690

Seaham

R South Tyne

Alston

34

CUMBRIA

Wearhead

R Wear

Tow Law

A692 A691

Durham

Peterlee

A167

Crook

N

0   20
km
0   10 miles

Much of the walk above Allenheads follows shooters' tracks (Walk 34)

INTRODUCTION

Northumberland – a land of open spaces and big skies

There's something very special about walking in Northumberland. It's got a lot to do with all the history in the landscape – from cliff-top castles and world-class Roman remains to long-abandoned prehistoric settlements hidden in the hills. It's also got something to do with those big northern skies, largely free of pollution, unfettered by man-made constructions and opening up views that stretch on for miles and miles and miles… It's undoubtedly got a lot to do with the landscape itself: remote hills, seemingly endless beaches, wild moors, dramatic geological features and valleys that are so mesmerizingly beautiful they defy description. It's surely related to the wildlife, too – from the feral goats and the upland birds that are sometimes the walkers' sole companions to the ancient woods and vast expanses of heather moorland that burst into vibrant purple bloom every summer.

Stretching from Berwick-upon-Tweed in the northeast to Haltwhistle in the southwest – two places that, even as the crow flies, are about 95km apart – Northumberland covers more than 5000km^2. It's not quite the biggest county in England, but as you wander its hills and valleys and beaches it feels like it. There are wide, open spaces here like no others found south of the border. Unsurprisingly, this is England's most sparsely populated county – with just 62 people per km^2. To put that into perspective, it compares with 73 in neighbouring Cumbria with its vast areas of uninhabited fell and moorland, or, at the other extreme, 3142 in the West Midlands and 5521 in Greater London. Want to escape from it all? This is the place to come!

Roughly 25 per cent of the county, including Hadrian's Wall and the Cheviot Hills, is protected within the boundaries of the Northumberland National Park. The county also has two designated Areas of Outstanding Natural Beauty – the Northumberland Coast and the North Pennines.

This book covers the whole county. The routes range from easy ambles on the coast and gentle woodland trails to long days out on the lonely hills: hopefully, something for all types of walker – and all types of weather.

WEATHER

Like the rest of the UK, Northumberland experiences plenty of meteorological variety but, being on the east side of an island dominated by moisture-laden southwesterlies, it tends to be drier and generally more benign than the western side. Having said that, the Pennines and the Cheviot Hills get more than their fair share of strong winds, heavy rain and snow. And, in winter, the easterly winds that periodically come in off the North Sea are enough to bring tears to your eyes. During summer, the coast is prone to sea fog, or haar, an annoyance that will normally burn off quickly, but can linger all day if there's a steady wind coming off the North Sea to keep replenishing the banks of moisture.

It's shorts weather above Rothbury!

Now for the statistics. July and August are the warmest months, with a mean daily maximum temperature of about 18°C. The coldest months are January and February with a mean daily minimum of 1.5°C. According to rainfall totals for Boulmer on the coast, the wettest period is from October to December, while April to July are the driest months. Obviously these figures will differ according to altitude, as well as latitude and longitude; and don't forget, they're averages.

Snow is even more widely varied from one part of the county to another – with the white stuff rarely lying for long on the coast while, in the North Pennines, it'd be an unusual winter if there weren't occasional road closures. Generally speaking, January and February see the most, although snow can fall any time from late October to late April in the North Pennines and, to a lesser extent, in the Cheviot Hills.

The weather becomes an important consideration when heading on to the high ground, particularly in winter. Check forecasts before setting out, and prepare accordingly. The Mountain Weather Information Service (www.mwis.org.uk) covers the higher Cheviot Hills in its Southern Uplands forecast for Scotland, while the Meteorological Office (www. metoffice.gov.uk) provides detailed predictions for locations throughout the county.

GEOLOGY

Northumberland's size gives rise to a varied and complex underlying geology. In its most simplistic form, it could be summed up as a mixture of largely Carboniferous sedimentary rocks and volcanic rocks, both intrusive and extrusive, all topped by Quaternary deposits, including those of the last glacial period.

The rolling hills of the Cheviot range are generally associated with a period of mountain building known as the Caledonian Orogeny, about 490 to 390 million years ago. The collision of several mini-continents, including Avalonia, with Laurentia and the subduction of the Iapetus Ocean, resulted in volcanic activity. This created a mass of granite surrounded by extrusive volcanic rocks, most notably andesite. The collision of the plates also resulted in faulting, evident in places such as the Harthope and Breamish valleys.

Although there are older rocks dating as far back as the Ordovician, about 450 million years ago, the rocks of the North Pennines are largely Carboniferous limestone, sandstones and shales laid down about 360–300 million years ago, when this area was covered by a tropical sea.

There are certain surface features that will stand out as walkers explore the county – the andesite outcrops that form small crags on the otherwise smooth slopes of the Cheviot Hills; the fell sandstones, most prominent on the Simonside Hills; and, probably

Hadrian's Wall was built on the Great Whin Sill

most famously, the dolerite of the Great Whin Sill, on which Hadrian's Wall and several castles were built. The latter was formed towards the end of the Carboniferous period, when movement of tectonic plates forced magma to be squeezed sideways between beds of existing rock. The magma, as it then slowly cooled, crystallised and shrank, forming hexagonal columns.

WILDLIFE AND HABITATS

With habitats covering anything from coastal dunes to 600m-plus hills, it's not surprising that the wildlife of Northumberland is extremely diverse. While walking the coast, keep your eyes peeled for seals and even the occasional dolphin out at sea. Seals often haul out on the sands of the Lindisfarne National Nature Reserve (see Walk 4), while dolphins have frequently been spotted playing in the waters around Berwick. Seabirds such as puffins, guillemots, Arctic terns and shags nest on the rocky Farne Islands, while winter visitors to the coast include barnacle geese, brent geese, pink-footed geese, wigeon, grey plovers and bar-tailed godwits. The waders, in particular, enjoy feeding on the sand and mudflats, where they are joined by their British cousins, who abandon the hills for a winter holiday at the seaside.

At first sight, the delicate and ever-shifting dunes seem to be home to nothing more than marram grass; closer inspection reveals an array of wildflowers such as lady's bedstraw, bloody cranesbill, houndstongue, bird's foot trefoil and restharrow.

They're also home to common lizards and an assortment of moths and butterflies, including the dark green fritillary and grayling.

Moving inland, the uplands contain some very important ecosystems. Almost 30 per cent of England's blanket bog is found in the North Pennines, home to peat-building sphagnum moss as well as heather, bog asphodel, bilberry, crowberry and cotton grass. Rare Arctic/alpine plants, such as cloudberry, still thrive on the highest moors. The nutrient-poor, acidic soils also support native grasses such as purple moor grass, mat-grass and wavy-hair grass, which give the Cheviot Hills, beyond the heavily managed grouse moors, their distinctive look.

The North Pennines and Cheviot Hills are important for a variety of bird species, including red grouse, some of England's last remaining populations of elusive black grouse, and the heavily persecuted and extremely rare hen harrier, as well as merlin, kestrel, short-eared owl, peregrine falcon, ring ouzel, skylark, lapwing, golden plover, whinchat and wheatear.

As far as mammals go, the most common species you're likely to see on the uplands is sheep, but there is wildlife too – foxes, brown hares, weasels and stoats can be seen, particularly around dusk and dawn. Small bands of feral goats also roam parts of the Cheviot Hills.

The valleys and low-lying woods are home to badgers, roe deer, voles, shrews, minks and otters. Northumberland is also one of England's last bastions of native red squirrels, driven to extinction in other

Curlew in flight

Feral goat in the Cheviot Hills

parts of the country by the introduced grey squirrel. Herons, kingfishers and dippers can often be spotted along the burns, and the woods are home to wagtails, long-tailed tits, great spotted woodpeckers, cuckoos, siskin, redpolls, finches and warblers, among others. Buzzards are probably the most common of the raptors, but any of the species found on the uplands, with the exception of the hen harrier, can also be spotted at lower altitudes.

Walkers should be aware that, as in most of the UK, there's always a chance of stumbling across adders, our only venomous snake. They're most likely to be spotted on warm days, basking out in the open – sometimes on tracks and paths. Don't be too alarmed: the adder will usually make itself scarce as soon as it senses your approach. They bite only as a last resort – if you tread on one or try to pick one up. Even then, for most people, the worst symptoms of an adder

Adders are the UK's only poisonous snakes

bite are likely to be nausea and severe bruising, although medical advice should be sought immediately. It's a different story for our canine friends: an adder bite can kill dogs.

HISTORY

People have been leaving their mark on Northumberland's landscape for millennia. There is even evidence of Mesolithic hunter-gatherers – in the form of a dwelling at Howick (see Walk 1) and small pieces of worked flint in Allendale. But it was really only in Neolithic times that human beings, farming for the first time, began to have a more profound impact on the landscape. Suddenly, after centuries of being left to their own devices, the forests that had slowly colonised the land after the departure of the last ice sheets were under threat as trees made way for crops and livestock.

By the Bronze Age – roughly 2500BC to about 800BC – people were not only developing the first field systems seen in Britain, they were also using metallurgy to create tools and ornaments. There are Bronze Age remains scattered throughout the county, most notably burial cairns, stone circles and the prolific cup-and-ring marks found on boulders. This 'rock art' was made by Neolithic and early Bronze Age people between 6000 and 3500 years ago, but its meaning has been lost in the intervening centuries.

Several walks in this book take in some of these important prehistoric sites, but there are others well worth visiting such as the 4200-year-old

Duddo Stone Circle

Rock art at Routin Linn

Duddo Stone Circle a few kilometres southeast of Norham, and Routin Linn, the largest decorated rock in England. A few kilometres east of the historic village of Ford, it's covered in dozens of carvings and can't fail to impress.

The Iron Age, starting in Britain in roughly 800BC and lasting up until the arrival of the Romans, gave us the hillforts that today dot the Cheviot Hills. These were built by the Votadini, a tribe of Celts that lived in an area of southeast Scotland and northeast England from the Firth of Forth down to the River Tyne. When the Romans arrived, the Votadini were at first ruled directly. After Hadrian's Wall was built, and the Romans retreated south, this tribe remained allied with the invaders and formed a 'friendly' buffer

between the legionaries and the Pictish tribes further north.

The Romans left Northumberland with its most famous historic feature – Hadrian's Wall. In AD122, while on a visit to Britain, the Emperor Hadrian ordered a defensive wall to be built against the Pictish people. Over the next six years, professional soldiers, or legionaries, built a wall almost 5m high and 80 Roman miles (73 modern miles) long, from Wallsend in the east to Bowness-on-Solway in the west. Some of the best-preserved remaining stretches of the wall, as well as forts and other settlements associated with it, feature prominently in several walks in this book.

The departure of the Romans in the early part of the fifth century left something of a vacuum in terms of government and leadership in much of Britain. Germanic settlers, namely the Angles and Saxons, were happy to step into the breach. The first known Anglian king of the area that includes modern-day Northumberland was Ida, who ruled from about AD547. Later, his kingdom, Bernicia, united with the neighbouring Deira to form the powerful Northumbria. Now began something of a 'golden age' for the region: a time of peace when religion, culture, art and learning flourished. This was the time of King Oswald, the Irish monk Aidan, Lindisfarne's Bishop Cuthbert (see Walk 4) and the great scholar Bede, all later venerated as saints. The peace was shortlived, however: in AD793 Vikings desecrated Lindisfarne in one of their first attacks on the British Isles.

Following William the Conqueror's brutal Harrying of the North, when tens of thousands of people were killed, the Normans rebuilt several Anglian monasteries, including Lindisfarne; they established a number of new abbeys, including at Alnwick and Blanchland, and built castles at Newcastle, Warkworth, Alnwick, Bamburgh, Norham and Dunstanburgh, to name but a few.

But, of course, Northumberland remained a frontier region – peace was a rare thing. Castles and territory passed from English rule to Scottish rule and back again. In 1314 Scots, led by Robert the Bruce, ransacked the north of England – towns were burned, churches destroyed and villagers slaughtered. And then there were the infamous Border Reivers, the lawless clans that went about looting and pillaging throughout the border regions. These ruthless families, owing

Roman ruins at Housesteads Fort (Walk 30)

19

Scottish forces captured Norham Castle four times (Walk 6)

Dunstanburgh Castle (Walk 2)

allegiance to neither crown, brought new, bleak words such as 'bereaved' and 'blackmail' to the English language and created the need for bastles (see Walk 22), pele towers and other defensive structures. Life really only began to settle down in 1603, when James VI of Scotland became the first ruler of both England and Scotland.

Northumberland's mineral wealth and the presence of a large port at Newcastle led to significant developments in trade and industry. Lead was mined for centuries at Allendale and Blanchland (see walks 33–36), the most prosperous period being the 18th and 19th centuries, but it was coal that really fuelled the area's economic development. The Romans were known to use this carbon-based mineral, but it was only in the 12th and 13th centuries that the industry

took off – with significant amounts of coal being exported to London via Newcastle. Come the Industrial Revolution and things really began to hot up: there were about 10,000 colliers in northeast England by 1810. With coal came the railways – some of the great pioneers of rail and steam, including George Stephenson, originated from Northumberland.

WHERE TO STAY

Tourism is an important part of Northumberland's economy and, as such, the county is well served by accommodation providers and dining facilities. Budget travellers may want to consider youth hostels, camping or other self-catering options, although many of these close for at least part of the winter.

Rothbury makes a good base for several of the walks in this book

The best bases for walks in this book are Wooler, Rothbury, Alwinton, Seahouses, Craster, Belford, Berwick-upon-Tweed, Haltwhistle, Kielder, Blanchland and Allendale Town.

PUBLIC TRANSPORT

Rural dwellers will probably regard Northumberland as being reasonably well served by public transport; but, if you live in a large city, you're in for a shock. Most of the start points for walks in this book are served by public transport – even Alwinton and Harbottle high up in Coquetdale have regular buses. But regular doesn't always mean frequent: if you miss your bus, don't expect another one to come along in half an hour. In fact, if

you miss the Coquetdale Circular, you might have to wait several days for the next one. Having said that, the few linear walks in the book are served by regular and reasonably frequent buses.

Two railways in the national network pass through Northumberland: the East Coast Main Line and the Tyne Valley Line. As well as serving Newcastle, some trains on the former stop at Morpeth, Alnwick and Morpeth. Tyne Valley trains between Carlisle and Newcastle stop at Haltwhistle, Hexham, Prudhoe and several other smaller towns and villages.

If you're planning to use public transport, the best resource is Traveline – 0871 200 2233 or www. traveline.info.

MAPS

The map extracts in this book are from the Ordnance Survey's 1:50,000 Landranger series. They are meant as a guide only, and walkers are advised to purchase the relevant map(s) – and know how to navigate using them. To complete all the walks, you'll need Landranger sheets 74, 75, 80, 81, 86 and 87. The OS 1:25,000 Explorer series provides greater detail, showing field boundaries as well as access land. Sheets OL16, OL31, OL42, OL43, 332, 340, 339 and 346 cover all the routes in this book.

WAYMARKING AND ACCESS

Many of the routes in this book are well signposted – even on the highest of the Cheviot Hills, you'll come across occasional fingerposts. Some follow sections of long-distance paths, most of which have additional waymarking. The Pennine Way and Hadrian's Wall Path, for example, are marked by the white acorn symbols of the National Trails, while paths such as St Cuthbert's Way and St Oswald's Way have their own signage.

As well as thousands of kilometres of bridleways and footpaths, there are huge tracts of access land where people have the right to roam without having to stick rigidly to rights of way. These are, however, subject to restrictions, including short-term closures to the general public and complete dog bans (see below).

There are tens of thousands of hectares of Forestry Commission land throughout Northumberland, as well as privately owned commercial forests, so it's almost inevitable

Fingerposts exist even high in the Cheviot Hills

that, at some point, you'll come across forestry operations involving heavy machinery. Often, walkers are simply advised to exercise caution; occasionally, paths will be diverted or whole sections of access land will be temporarily closed. In these cases, watch carefully for signs telling you what to do.

DOGS

Most of the walks in this book follow public rights of way from start to finish and, as such, there are no restrictions on dog access. However, where a route crosses access land but is not on a right of way, walkers need to check access rights. The landowner has a right to ban dogs, usually for reasons relating to grouse moorland management. Restrictions are subject to change and can be found on Natural England's CRoW and coastal access maps at www. openaccess.naturalengland.org.uk.

Dog owners should always be sensitive to the needs of livestock and wildlife. The law states that dogs have to be controlled so that they do not scare or disturb livestock or wildlife, including ground-nesting birds. On access land, they have to be kept on leads of no more than 2m long from 1 March to 31 July – and all year round near sheep. A dog chasing lambing sheep can cause them to abort. Remember that, as a last resort, farmers can shoot dogs to protect their livestock.

Cattle, particularly cows with calves, may very occasionally pose a risk to walkers with dogs. If you ever feel threatened by cattle, let go of your dog's lead and let it run free.

People are discouraged from walking on Hadrian's Wall, but terrier Jess thinks she's seen a sheep

Walkers need to be able to use a map and compass

CLOTHING, EQUIPMENT AND SAFETY

The amount of gear you take on a walk and the clothes you wear will differ according to the length of the route, the time of year and the terrain you're likely to encounter. Preparing for the Border Ridge and The Cheviot in the height of winter, for example, requires more thought than when setting out on a walk from Craster. As such, this section is aimed primarily at those heading out in the winter or venturing on to high ground.

Even in the height of summer, your daysack should contain wind- and waterproof gear. Most people will also carry several layers of clothing – this is more important if you are heading on to higher ground, where the weather is prone to sudden change.

As far as footwear goes, some walkers like good, solid leather boots with plenty of ankle support, while others prefer something lighter.

Every walker needs to carry a map and compass – and know how to use them. Always take food and water with you – enough to sustain you during the walk, plus extra rations in case you're out for longer than originally planned. Emergency equipment should include a whistle and a torch – the distress signal being six flashes/whistle-blasts repeated at one-minute intervals. Pack a small first aid kit, too.

Carry a fully charged mobile telephone, but use it to summon help on the hills only in a genuine emergency. If things do go badly wrong and you need help, first make sure you have a note of all the relevant details such as your location, the nature of the injury/ problem, the number of people in the party and your mobile phone number. Only then should you dial 999 and ask for police, then mountain rescue.

USING THIS GUIDE

The walks in this book are divided into five geographical areas: north-east Northumberland, covering the area between the Cheviot Hills and the North Sea coast; National Park (north), covering the Cheviot Hills and the area around Rothbury; Kielder, including forest walks, lakeside walks and hill walks; Tyne Valley and National Park (south), an area that takes in Hadrian's Wall; and the North Pennines. All walks start in Northumberland, but one crosses the border into Scotland (Walk 5) and one briefly flirts with Cumbria (Walk 32).

Most of the routes are circular, but there are a few linear walks that make use of local bus services. Check timetables carefully to make sure you have enough time to complete the route.

Each walk description contains information on start/finish points, distance covered, total ascent, grade, approximate walking time, terrain, maps required, facilities (public toilets and refreshments) and transport options. The walks are graded one to five, one being the easiest. Please note that these ratings are subjective, based not just on distance and total ascent, but also the terrain encountered. Walkers are advised to read route descriptions before setting out to get a better idea of what to expect. It might be a good idea to do a relatively easy walk first and then judge the rest accordingly.

On the beach near Howick (Walk 1)

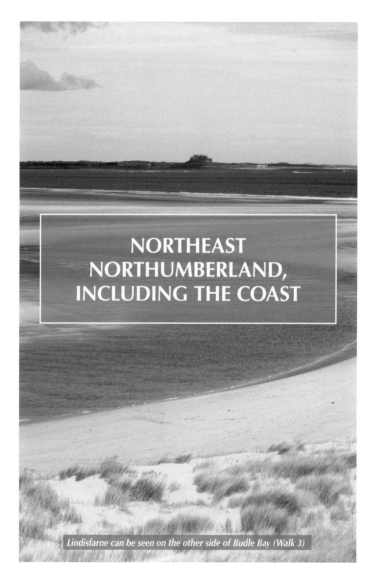

NORTHEAST NORTHUMBERLAND, INCLUDING THE COAST

Lindisfarne can be seen on the other side of Budle Bay (Walk 3)

WALK 1
Craster and Howick Hall

Start/finish	Craster Quarry car park, Craster (NU 256 197)
Distance	9.2km (5¾ miles)
Total ascent	137m (450ft)
Grade	1
Walking time	2½hr
Terrain	Field paths, road, track, low cliffs
Maps	OS Explorer 332; OS Landranger 81
Transport	Buses 418 and X18
Facilities	Craster Seafood Restaurant, Jolly Fisherman and Shoreline Café, all in Craster; public toilets and seasonal catering van in car park

Starting from the attractive fishing village of Craster, this relaxing amble heads south to Howick Hall before taking to roads and rough tracks to reach the coast path and a gentle stroll back to the village. Even across the farmland at the start of the walk, the paths are generally easy to follow. Unwind and enjoy a few undemanding hours on this gorgeous section of the coast!

From the car park, take the footpath heading southwest towards Craster South Farm – along the edge of the Northumberland Wildlife Trust's Arnold Memorial Nature Reserve. Having ignored one path to the right, you'll quickly reach a kissing-gate providing access to more open ground. Follow the faint trail away from the woods (southwest). After a slight rise, stay parallel with a fence over to the left.

Reaching a road, cross diagonally right to head up a lane – signposted Howick Hall Gates. The lane ends in a turning circle at **Craster South Farm**. Just before this, bear left around the side of a farm gate. The muddy path soon joins a more solid track from the left. Continue with the field boundary on your left for almost 500m. Having crossed another rough track, go through a kissing-gate.

Still following signs for Howick Hall, bear half-right, aiming for a farm gate at the base of the low crags of **Hips Heugh**. Once through the gate, skirt the base of the rocks for another 100m or so and then swing right across damp ground to go through a kissing-gate next to a ladder stile. A fingerpost shows the way through the crops ahead (south-southwest).

In the field corner, a pair of gates with a bridge between them provides access to the next field. Keep close to the trees on the right until you encounter a clear track rising through the woods. Follow this up to a broad, stony track near the walls of **Howick Hall**. This leads to a road, along which you turn left.

Howick Hall has been owned by the Grey family since 1319, although the house was rebuilt in 1928 after a massive fire. Among the many Greys who have lived there, the most distinguished is probably Charles, the second Earl Grey, after whom the bergamot-flavoured tea is named. As leader of the Whigs, he was Prime Minister from 1830 to 1834, during the time of the Great Reform Act 1932. The grounds – but not the house – are open to the public. They are particularly famed for their dense banks of snowdrops in late winter and

The coast south of Craster

For the first time on this walk you're able to look south along the coast, towards a series of small, golden beaches cradled by long fingers of rock.

their unusual range of trees, gathered from some of the farthest-flung corners of the world. Visit www. howickhallgardens.org for more information.

After 850m the road bends sharp left. Take the track on the right here – signposted Alnmouth via coast path. At the entrance to **Sea Houses** Farm, keep straight on – along what is now a public byway. ◄

A small, fenced **enclosure** to the left of the track was the site of an archaeological dig from 2000 to 2002, when a rare example of a Mesolithic hut was unearthed. Radiocarbon dating from hearths inside the home show it was built in about 7800BC, making it Northumberland's oldest occupied site and among the oldest in the UK. Five Bronze Age burial cists were also found.

Just before the track drops to Howick Burn, a small gate on the right allows a 250m detour to the earthwork remains of an Iron Age settlement. After a metal gate, the mouth of Howick Burn is reached – a chance, finally, to enjoy a paddle in the chilly North Sea, or to search for fossils. Turn sharp left immediately after the gate – almost back on yourself – along the coast path as it hugs the top of low cliffs.

> The lump of metal on the rocks below in a short while is part of the boiler of the French steam trawler **Tadorne**, which ran aground here in 1913. Five of the crew were killed in the accident, but another 25 were rescued by the Boulmer lifeboat.

The path goes through a couple of gates, passes to the seaward side of Sea Houses Farm and reaches a junction with a more solid path. Turn right along this. Views of Dunstanburgh Castle, further up the coast, come and go until you round **Cullernose Point**; now, the ruins take on a more surreal appearance, looming mirage-like above Craster.

Passing through a kissing-gate, keep to the seaward side of the first buildings on the southern edge of the village. The path passes to the right of a play area. After a set of steps, the coast path enters the beer garden behind the Jolly Fisherman pub. After a gate on the other side, turn left along a track between the buildings. Go left at the road and then take the lane rising on the right – Whin Hill. Swing right at the top and then follow the narrower path to the left. This leads back to the car park.

The fishing village of Craster

WALK 2
Dunstanburgh Castle and Low Newton

Start/finish	Craster Quarry pay-and-display car park, Craster (NU 256 197)
Distance	12.4km (7¾ miles)
Total ascent	165m (541ft)
Grade	1
Walking time	3½hr
Terrain	Coastal paths, mostly grass but sometimes in dunes; sandy beach
Maps	OS Explorer 332 and 340; OS Landranger 75 and 81
Transport	Buses 418 and X18
Facilities	Craster Seafood Restaurant, Jolly Fisherman and Shoreline Café, Craster; public toilets and seasonal catering van in Craster Quarry car park; Ship Inn and public toilets in Low Newton; Dunstanburgh Castle Golf Course Clubhouse

Looming spectre-like over the tiny harbour village of Craster, the spectacular cliff-top ruins of Dunstanburgh Castle form the focus of much of this walk. Taking the form of a double figure-of-eight, the route explores a narrow coastal margin north of the village as far as Low Newton-by-the-Sea, a pretty gathering of 18th-century fishermen's cottages now owned by the National Trust. Here, at the half-way mark, you'll also find the Ship Inn – a great spot to break the route before your return journey.

The site is well worth visiting if you're here during opening hours. Admission is free to members of both English Heritage and the National Trust.

From the entrance to the car park, turn right along the road. Reaching the edge of Craster's harbour, take the lane on the left – signposted Dunstanburgh Castle. Beyond the road-end gate, keep close to the sea as you walk along the close-cropped turf. Unfortunately, there isn't a way round **Dunstanburgh Castle** on its seaward side, so you'll need to head slightly inland as you near its fenced compound. ◄

Occupying a windswept headland of Whin Sill rock, **Dunstanburgh Castle** is one of England's dramatically situated castles. Dating back to 1313, it was built by Earl Thomas of Lancaster, probably as a show of might in his opposition to King Edward II. The only time it saw military action was during the Wars of the Roses in the second half of the 15th century, when it was captured twice by Yorkist forces.

Dunstanburgh Castle dominates the landscape around Craster

Having passed to the left of the castle mound, the path heads back towards the sea and through a gate.

The unusual rock formation jutting out into the North Sea here is known as the **Greymare Rock**. It consists of several layers of limestone warped by the heat and pressure caused by the same volcanic activity that created the Great Whin Sill.

Follow the trail along the seaward edge of the golf course, with **Embleton Bay** on the right.

There are several concrete **pillboxes** in Embleton Bay. Built in the early years of World War Two, these

33

were fitted with loopholes through which weapons could be fired in the event of an attempted invasion.

On reaching the sand dunes, you have a choice. You can drop on to the beach here and follow it for 2.3km to Low Newton, or to avoid getting feet wet on the crossing of Embleton Burn as it enters the sea, you can continue through the dunes for now. If choosing the latter option, the trail will later cross a footbridge. Ignore a second bridge on the right. Then, at a gap in the dunes, head on to the beach and walk north along the golden sand for 1.5km to **Low Newton-by-the-sea**.

The beach ends as you reach the buildings at Low Newton. Where the path comes in from the beach, cross the road and take the signposted coastal path along the narrow lane opposite. Just before the toilet block, follow the lane round to the left. The narrowing path passes to the left of Risemoor Cottage and then skirts the edge of Newton Pool Nature Reserve. At a sign announcing your return to the golf course, keep left along the clear path. The dunes here are dotted with wooden chalets built in the 1930s.

On reaching the bridge over Embleton Burn ignored earlier in the walk, turn right along a broad path through the golf course. About 130m beyond the bridge, turn left

– signposted Craster. After crossing a footbridge, head right to continue along the course's rough, western fringe. Continue past the gate at the **Dunstan Steads** road-end, aiming all the while for Dunstanburgh Castle again. You'll encounter a golfers' track to the left. Keep right here and then, on reaching the furthest green, leave the fence and head left to rejoin the trail along the coastal edge. Briefly retracing your steps from earlier, follow the path along the base of the castle rocks, but then keep right at two forks. The path crosses a bridge of sorts close to some gorse-covered rocks and makes its way back towards the sea. Go through the gate, keep to the coastal trail for about 80m and then, as the fence on the left ends, head up to the right on a faint line through the grass.

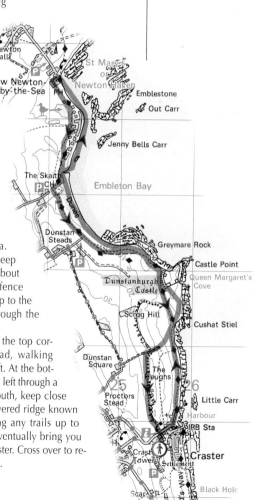

Beyond the stile in the top corner, keep straight ahead, walking with a fence on your left. At the bottom of a stony track, turn left through a kissing-gate. Walking south, keep close to the base of gorse-covered ridge known as **The Heughs**. Ignoring any trails up to the left, this path will eventually bring you out on the road into Craster. Cross over to re-enter the quarry car park.

WALK 3

Seahouses to Belford

Start	War Memorial roundabout, centre of Seahouses (NU 219 320)
Finish	Market cross in Belford (NU 108 339)
Distance	17.2km (10¾ miles)
Total ascent	310m (1017ft)
Grade	2
Walking time	4¾hr
Terrain	Dunes and beach; golf course; farm paths; quiet country lanes; the walk also involves crossing the East Coast Main Line and the busy A1
Maps	OS Explorer 340; OS Landranger 75
Transport	The start and finish points are linked by buses 418 and X18
Facilities	Several cafés and pubs in Seahouses, Bamburgh and Belford; public toilets in Seahouses, near start of walk, and slightly off route in Bamburgh

This linear walk makes use of buses linking Belford and Seahouses. Starting from the latter, the route heads northwest to Bamburgh: at any time other than high tide, this means several wonderful kilometres of beach walking on firm sand. After passing beneath the massive walls of Bamburgh Castle, the route heads into the village – an opportunity for a pub lunch or just a coffee-and-cake stop – before picking up the route of the St Oswald's Way. A stunning perspective on Budle Bay and the sands leading towards Lindisfarne provide an impressive end to the coastal section of the walk. The route now heads inland across rolling farmland and through woods to reach the attractive village of Belford.

From the War Memorial roundabout in Seahouses, head northwest along the coast road – the B1340. After a few hundred metres, step off the pavement to follow a path along the top of the low cliffs. This soon reaches the beach and the southern edge of **St Aidan's Dunes**. If

THE FARNE ISLANDS

The Farne Islands are clearly visible just off the coast. Consisting of 28 islands, the group is famous for its wildlife including grey seals, puffins, eider ducks, kittiwakes, fulmars, shags, sandwich terns, common terns, guillemots and razorbills. From the 7th century onwards, several monks, including St Aidan and St Cuthbert, used the islands as a hermitage. A formal cell of Benedictine monks was established here in the mid-13th century.

In more modern times, the islands became home to lighthouse keepers. Among these were William Darling and his daughter Grace who, in 1838, carried out a daring sea rescue which resulted in Grace becoming a national heroine. During stormy seas, the Darlings had spotted the wreck of the paddle steamship, the Forfarshire, on a nearby island. Believing that conditions were too rough for the lifeboat to be launched, they set out in a rowing boat and managed to rescue the nine survivors. Grace's role in the heroic feat became famous: Wordsworth wrote a poem about her, portrait artists flocked to the island to paint her, later folk singers wrote songs about her and, when she became ill with tuberculosis, the Duchess of Northumberland tended to her in person.

Today, no humans live permanently on the islands, although there are National Trust wardens resident for nine months of the year. Boat trips run from Seahouses.

the tide's out, you can walk the beach all the way to Bamburgh. Alternatively, you can follow a trail through the dunes.

On reaching the next buildings at **Monks House**, if the tide's high, you might have to head back up on to the B1340 by following the right-of-way to the left of the buildings. If you do, turn right along the grass verge. After 900m – almost opposite the farm track up to Greenhills – go through a gap in

map continues
on page 39

the fence on the right to follow a trail through the dunes and back to the beach.

Eventually, you'll pass beneath the walls of **Bamburgh Castle**. Drawing level with the old windmill at the northwest end of the castle precinct, head into the dunes, aiming for the castle walls. Reaching some fence posts, turn right – following signs for the village. Bear left at a fork and then follow the path around either side of the cricket pitch to reach the **B1340** again.

The core of **Bamburgh Castle** dates from the 11th century, but there had been a stronghold on the site for many centuries before the Normans arrived. Indeed, in the middle of the 6th century, the Anglo-Saxon king Ida ruled over the kingdom of Bernicia from here. The castle was bought in the 19th century by William Armstrong, the Tyneside industrialist who built Cragside near Rothbury. His descendants still live in the castle today, although parts of the building are open to the public.

Bamburgh Castle

map continues
on page 41

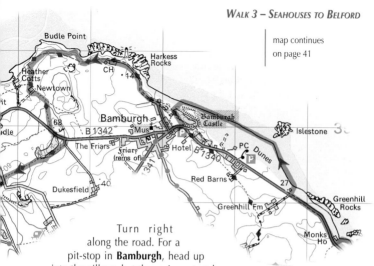

Turn right
along the road. For a
pit-stop in **Bamburgh**, head up
into the village, but the main route takes
the next turning on the right – The Wynding. This
ends at Bamburgh Castle Golf Course.

Following the route of St Oswald's Way and the
Northumberland Coast Path – all the way to Belford,
in fact – head through the gate on to the golf course.
A series of blue-topped posts leads the way across the
course, mostly keeping to its seaward side. ▶

As you pass around the back of a concrete pill-box,
follow the St Oswald's Way up to the left. Blue-topped
posts lead across the western edge of the golf course. Just
after a kissing-gate, turn left along the surfaced lane for
about 70m. Go through the large gate set back on the
left. A broad, grassy path passes to the right of the buildings at **Newtown**. On reaching a track T-junction, head to
the fence over to the left and follow it up the side of the
field. Beyond the next kissing-gate, you're back on the
golf course again. Bear slightly right to follow the now
familiar blue-topped posts south-southeast to a small
wooden gate.

Turn left along the **B1342** and take the next road on
the right – signposted Dukesfield. In just a few metres,
go through a kissing-gate on the right – signposted

You'll soon be able to
look straight across
Budle Bay to the
long stretch of beach
at Ross Back Sands,
leading almost all the
way to Lindisfarne.

Looking across Budle Bay to Lindisfarne

Spindlestone Heughs. The route now heads roughly southwest across the farmland. There's a faint path on the ground and lots of waymarked stiles to guide the way.

Reaching a minor road, turn left and immediately right, towards the Waren holiday park. Follow this lane round to the left and then watch for a footpath signposted to the right. Skirting the edge of the caravan site, the route keeps close to the hedge on your left. Don't be tempted to follow the access lane up to the right; instead, pass through a small gate to continue in the same direction but now with a walled area of woodland on your right. After dropping through some trees close to the base of the crags of Spindlestone Heughs, the route passes out into a meadow. After the next gate, keep close to the fence on your right until the path enters some woods. A clear, beaten-earth trail leads down through the trees to a quiet lane.

Turn left through the charming, wooded valley of Waren Burn where, in spring, the smell of wild garlic fills the air. At a T-junction opposite Spindlestone Mill, turn right. Follow the road round to the right beyond the Outchester Ducket, a distinctive tower marked on some maps as a **windmill**. Go right at the T-junction and then take the next lane on the left. Follow this for 350m and then go through the wooden gate on the left – signed Station Cottages and Belford.

Keep close to the field boundary on the left until you reach a ladder stile. Cross this, turn right to walk beside the wall for a short while and then swing left. After the next gate, go straight through the field, following overhead power lines. Maintain the same line along a rough track and then, when it bends left, go through the gate straight ahead to continue with the power lines. After crossing a disused railway, bear left. The trail crosses some damp ground before reaching the East Coast Main Line. The railway has to be carefully crossed. Use the phone in the yellow box to check with the signalman that it's safe to do so. ▶

Don't take any chances: the trains reach speeds of more than 100mph along this stretch of line.

Aim immediately right of the main group of grain silos ahead. You'll go through a couple of small fields along the way before the path skirts the edge of the silo compound. Your next obstacle is the busy A1 road. It's only a single carriageway at this point on its journey from London to Edinburgh, but the traffic still moves fast, so be careful.

After the stile on the other side, maintain your line across the field. After a kissing-gate, go over the rough track to walk beside **Belford Burn**. Keep it on your right until you reach the B6349 on the edge of **Belford**. Turn right to walk up to the medieval market cross in the middle of the village.

WALK 4
Lindisfarne

Start/finish	First pay-and-display car park on the island (NU 126 424)
Distance	8.9km (5½ miles)
Total ascent	100m (328ft)
Grade	1
Walking time	2½hr
Terrain	Dunes, beaches and grassy foreshore; grassy path; short sections on road
Maps	OS Explorer 340; OS Landranger 75
Transport	Bus 477
Facilities	Several cafés and pubs on island; public toilets in smaller village car park

There's so much more to Lindisfarne than most visitors to the tiny island realise. As well as a spectacular castle and one of the most important ecclesiastical sites in Britain, it is also the location of a massive dune system and, at low tide, vast white beaches with hardly a soul on them – truly uplifting places to wander. This walk completes a circuit of the island, exploring the secret dunes – part of a National Nature Reserve – before heading for the more popular attractions on the southern side of the island. Consult tide timetables before attempting to cross the causeway leading to the island. And don't forget to bring your binoculars!

From the car park entrance, turn right along the road. Just before dropping to the causeway, take the footpath sign-posted through a gate on the right. With views over the causeway, a cropped-grass path runs beside a fence on the right at first. Bear left at a clear fork and then head northwest through the dunes to reach a lonely stretch of beach to the southwest of **Back Skerrs**. Heading east from here, you now have a choice: if the tide's out, you can keep to the beach and the rocks at the back of the beach until the rocky headland of **Snipe Point** forces you back into the dunes, or you can keep to the dunes from the outset. There are lots of trails through the reserve – simply pick your route, staying as close to the sea as you can.

> **Lindisfarne National Nature Reserve** covers a massive 3500 hectares. Rare orchids and butterflies thrive in the dunes, while, in the autumn, huge flocks of brent geese fly in from Svalbard to spend the winter on the salt marsh and mudflats.

From Snipe Point, you'll be able to see the white pyramid at Emmanuel Head to the southeast. Make for this, crossing the beach at Sandham on the way. Even on a warm summer's day, while visitors throng the castle and priory on the other side of the island, this beautiful stretch of sand is surprisingly quiet.

From **Emmanuel Head**, continue on the grassy path closest to the sea. This swings south to reach a wall corner. Turn right here and then, in 350m, go through the small gate on the left. Follow the raised path, known as

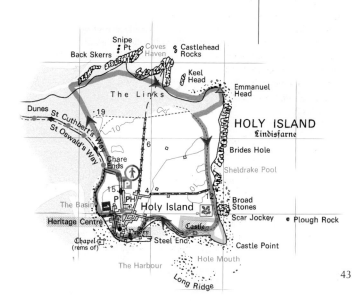

Emmanuel Head from the beach at Sandham

Watch for eider ducks as you near the sea again. These large, black-and-white sea ducks are sometimes known locally as Cuddy ducks, after St Cuthbert who forbade monks from eating or disturbing the birds.

the waggonway, along the eastern side of the island. It passes the bird hide beside The Lough – a good place to shelter on a wild day, or simply to watch the birds. As you head south, you can see the Farne Islands out at sea and Bamburgh Castle straight ahead. ◄ After passing through a gap in a wall, the waggonway swings right – making directly for Lindisfarne Castle. Crossing a bridge, it passes to the right of some substantial limekilns.

This complex and well-preserved set of **limekilns** was served by the waggonway along which you just walked. Limestone, quarried from the north of the island in the second half of the 19th century, was pulled in wheeled tubs to the kilns to be turned into quicklime. This was then exported to Scotland where it was used to make mortar, whitewash for walls and fertiliser.

The route passes directly below the **castle**'s northern ramparts and then out along the access lane.

Lindisfarne Castle was built as a fort in the middle of the 16th century, although it saw action only once – when it was briefly seized by Stuart supporters during the Jacobite Risings of 1715. It was rebuilt and refurbished in the Arts and Crafts style by the architect Edwin Lutyens between 1903 and 1906. Now owned by the National Trust, it was undergoing major restoration work at the time of writing.

Pass a small bay known as The Ouse. Drawing level with its western side, leave the lane by bearing left along the water's edge. Nearing some wooden sheds, bear right, ascending a surfaced path. This swings right to head out on to The Heugh, a little ridge of the Great Whin Sill. With good views of the priory, head to the far end of the ridge and descend the rocky path. After a few benches, go through a kissing-gate on the right. A path leads up to a quiet lane – opposite the entrance to St Mary's Church and a route into the **priory** grounds.

Lindisfarne Priory

WALKING IN NORTHUMBERLAND

LINDISFARNE PRIORY

A modern statue of St Aidan graces the site of the priory, but the island has become more closely associated with St Cuthbert. Briefly Bishop of Lindisfarne from AD685, he died in AD687. His body, miraculously undecayed 11 years after his death, caused the island to become a place of pilgrimage and strengthened its reputation as a place of great Christian learning.

In the early part of the 8th century the monks on the island, led by Bishop Eadrith, created the Lindisfarne Gospels. Lavishly illustrated and made from calfskin vellum, this masterpiece of early medieval art is now housed in the British Library in London. Its original bejewelled leather binding, replaced in the middle of the 19th century, is thought to have been lost during a Viking raid on the island.

Turn left along the lane. When you reach the school, turn left. Follow the fenced bridleway back towards the water's edge and turn right. If the tide's out, you can walk along the shore; if it's in, you'll have to keep close to the fence on the right, carefully negotiating the rabbit holes. On reaching the causeway road, turn right to return to the car park.

WALK 5
Berwick-upon-Tweed to Eyemouth

Start	Small parking area at the start of Berwick Pier (NU 005 527)
Finish	Bus stop beside Co-op's car park in Eyemouth (NT 944 644)
Distance	16.4km (10¼ miles)
Total ascent	595m (1950ft)
Grade	3
Walking time	5½hr
Terrain	Mostly cliff-top paths; field paths; quiet lanes
Maps	OS Explorer 346; OS Landranger 75 and 67 (both required)
Transport	Start and finish points are linked by buses 34, 60, 235, 236, 253 and 260
Facilities	Cafés and pubs in Berwick-upon-Tweed and Eyemouth; public toilets at Greens Haven

Much of Northumberland's coast is fairly flat, but this all changes north of Berwick-upon-Tweed. To sample the rugged cliffs of Berwickshire, this linear walk starts in Northumberland but later crosses the Scottish border to end in the attractive harbour town of Eyemouth. Relatively low-lying red sandstone cliffs give way to higher, more dramatic cliffs as the generally well-signposted Berwickshire Coast Path makes its way north.

This is the first of two walks in the book that venture beyond Northumberland's borders.

Head down the walled lane opposite the small parking area at the start of Berwick **Pier**. Follow it up a short slope and then, when it bends left, take the path on the right (no signpost). This heads out along the edge of the cliff-top golf course.

Soon after the Coastwatch lookout, you reach a junction of paths. Take the clear path to the right (not the one

map continues
on page 50

heading sharp right, which just leads to a golf tee). This leads to the Greens Haven car park, which has public toilets. Follow the car park's access lane inland for about 50m and then take the path on the right – not the surfaced path leading down into Fishermen's Haven, but the grassy path running along the seaward side of the **holiday park**'s low fence.

Eventually, the path and fence swing inland. Now watch for a fingerpost, where you turn sharp right to cross a bridge and return to the cliff-top proper – signposted Marshall Meadows. At the height of summer, this trail can be rather overgrown as its winds its way

Red sandstone cliffs near Berwick

along the top of the low cliffs. In spring and summer, watch for nesting fulmars and kittiwakes around the rocks of **Needles Eye**. These are only low cliffs, but there are a surprising number of caves cut into them as well as a few rocky pinnacles that are on their way to becoming off-shore stacks. It's a dramatic place to be on a wild day when the waves are battering the rocks below.

After a ladder stile, turn right along the main track through the **Marshall Meadows** holiday park. Keep left at any forks until you see a lane going left across the railway. Bear right here and keep right to follow a fenced path back out to the cliffs.

Before long, you reach a kissing-gate with the legend 'Failte gu Alba' on it. ▶

This is the Scottish border and the Gaelic sign translates simply as 'Welcome to Scotland'.

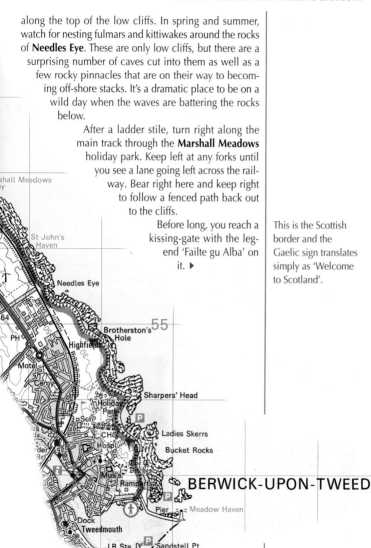

The remains of the **kirk at Lamberton**, just inland of here, is said to be the place where, in 1503, Margaret Tudor, the daughter of England's King Henry VII, was greeted by representatives of her new husband King James IV of Scotland. Her marriage paved the way, through her heirs, for the English and Scottish crowns to be united.

Once through the gate, as indicated by the waymarker, turn left and then follow the path round to the right. For the next few kilometres, as long as you keep the railway close by on your left, you can't really go wrong. Nature reserve panels provide information on species that can be found here, including butterflies, peregrine falcons, fulmars and badgers. Eventually, the path becomes more track-like and drops slightly. It's a little way in from the cliffs now as it skirts the base of a steep railway embankment.

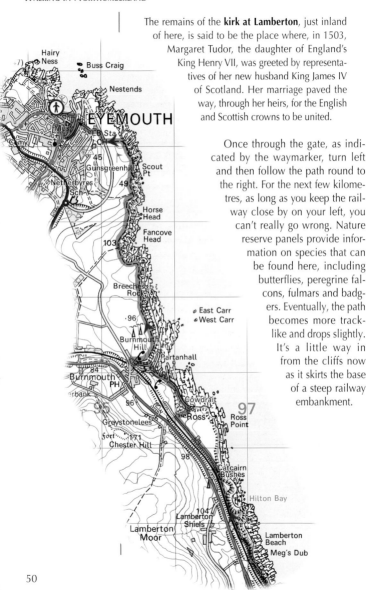

About 80m after passing above the buildings at Lamberton Holdings, descend the steps on the right to join a surfaced track heading in the same direction. Just before this swings left to pass under the railway, cross the stile next to the large metal gate on the right. Walk downhill beside the fence to a stile. Cross this and follow the switchback path down the steep cliff to the homes lining a narrow strip of land at the base of the cliffs at **Cowdrait**, meaning 'sheltered land'. Turn left along a lane in front of the beautifully situated homes.

The **bronze sculpture** on the harbour wall is by local artist Jill Watson. It shows the women and children left behind by the Black Friday disaster of October 14, 1881. This was the date of Scotland's biggest ever fishing disaster, when 189 men lost their lives during a ferocious storm. In total, 93 women were widowed and 267 children left without fathers.

Beyond the harbour in Lower **Burnmouth**, follow the road steeply uphill. Leave it at a left bend by taking the path to the right of the kirk. This winds its way up to a private road, along which you turn left. Turn right at the next road junction and then right again. You'll see a bus stop here should you wish to cut the walk short and catch the bus back to Berwick; otherwise, just before the village hall, take the surfaced track rising to the right. At a junction of routes in a short while, turn left and follow the path back out on to the cliffs.

As the coast path makes its way up on to Blaikie Heugh, it climbs beside a wall on the right. The top of this rise is at 103m above sea level and, as such, is the highest point on today's walk. At the highest point, the path switches to the seaward side of the wall. You're immediately greeted by the impressive cliffs and striking rock formations of Hurker's Haven. There's a bench here, so you can spend some time enjoying the scene.

The coast route briefly follows a broad, green ledge high above this tiny bay. Later crossing back to the other side of the wall, you're greeted by another fresh outlook: Eyemouth, day's end, has come into view. A gradual descent now begins. You'll soon see another golf course ahead. Ignore the first path signposted to the left just before you reach the edge of the course, but go through the rusty old kissing-gate at the next fingerpost – towards **Eyemouth**.

> You're now on the route of one of the **Border Brains Walks**, this one celebrating Alexander Dow. Born in Perthshire in 1736 but with strong Eyemouth links, he was one of the pioneers of European understanding of India's culture and history.

The clear trail cuts straight through the golf course to reach a road. Cross over and turn right for 150m. Immediately after an off-white building, go through the gap in the fence on the left (there's a footpath marker on a post.) Keep straight ahead, beside the building at first. You'll soon see a rough lane on the left. Heading in the same direction, join this and then turn right at a T-junction. Follow the road down and round to the left. Take the road descending right – towards a car park beside Gunsgreen House.

> **Gunsgreen House** was built in the middle of the 18th century for John Nisbet, a local 'free trader'. He was one of many merchants along this coast who made their fortunes from smuggling high-taxed goods such as brandy, tobacco, gin and tea. His home is full of hiding places where the contraband was stored.

At the bottom of the drop, go through a gap in the wall and cross the footbridge over a narrow waterway beside the harbour. Follow the walkway upstream, with Eye Water on your left and the harbour on the right. At the top end of the harbour area, turn right to follow Harbour Road. When it ends, bear left along Marine Parade and then walk along the seafront for about 200m – until you

pass behind the Co-op. The bus stop for the service back to Berwick is on the other side of the supermarket car park.

    When you get back to Berwick, make your way to the north bank of the River Tweed and then follow the waterway towards the sea – sometimes on little lanes, sometimes along the town walls. Eventually, you'll have to drop from the town walls on to Pier Road and follow this east to the car park where the walk started.

Eyemouth

WALK 6
Norham Castle and River Tweed

Start/finish	Arched entrance to Norham Castle grounds (NT 906 475). There's a small car park behind the castle; or park on roadside in village
Distance	10.8km (6¾ miles)
Total ascent	181m (595ft)
Grade	1/2
Walking time	3hr
Terrain	Fields, riverside paths, woodland and quiet roads; some sections overgrown in summer
Maps	OS Explorer 339; OS Landranger 74
Transport	Bus 67
Facilities	Mason's Arms and Victoria Hotel, Norham; public toilets near village hall

No book of walks in Northumberland would be complete without at least one walk along the River Tweed, the broad, majestic waterway that, in places, forms the border between England and Scotland. This figure-of-eight walk starts from the imposing ruins of Norham Castle before heading northeast beside the river. A combination of field and riverside paths make up the first loop, sometimes passing through woods that cling to the steep, often craggy embankment. The second, shorter and easier loop heads west along pleasant riverside paths before returning through the tranquil village of Norham.

From the castle entrance, walk down the road towards the village. After 150m, go through the kissing-gate on the right – signposted Horncliffe. At the bottom of the steps, with the River Tweed immediately in front of you, turn right. Just after a small ladder stile, bear left at a fork. This path climbs through the woods, overlooked in places by sandstone crags.

Having crossed two bridges, take the path heading up the slope on the right. After leaving the woods, turn

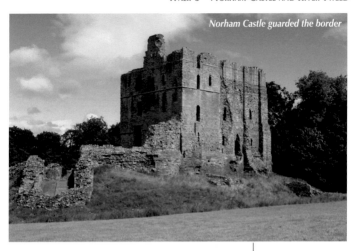

Norham Castle guarded the border

left along the field edge. Just before drawing level with the end of a hedgerow heading off to the right, the right-of-way crosses a stile on the left. It follows a narrow trail through the trees, over a dilapidated fence and then battles its way through knee-high vegetation to emerge onto **Hangman's Land**

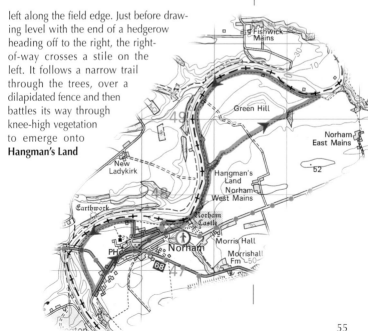

55

Some walkers have ignored the stile and created a vague path along the field edge to the right of the woodland.

a little further along the field edge that you just left. Turn left here. ◀

Just before reaching another fence/hedgerow heading right, drop left to cross a stile hidden, in summer, by long grass. Turn right to walk with the fence on your right. After the next stile, continue in roughly the same direction to cross two fields. On the far side of the second of these, bear right to descend with a fence on your left. Cross the stile in the bottom corner. Bear left and then right to keep close to the slope on the right. Where a grassy track swings right through a shallow gap in the hills, climb the slope immediately ahead (northeast).

Walking with a fence on your right now, you're now looking down on the River Tweed and the tiny, derelict building on St Thomas's Island. After the next stile, keep close to the field boundary on the left. Having battled your way through the vegetation for about 170m, watch carefully for a stile hidden behind the hedgerow on the left. Cross this and turn left along a clear path. After passing a bench, the path drops to cross a ladder stile. Beyond a second stile down in the field corner, you're on a path beside the River Tweed.

St Thomas's Island on the River Tweed

THE RIVER TWEED

The River Tweed is Europe's largest salmon rod fishery south of the Arctic Circle. As well as salmon, other fish including sea trout and brown trout are caught here. This section of the river falls within the Horncliffe beat and the white markers you'll see as you make your way upstream indicate each of the 20 named pools where fishing can take place – from the bank itself, by boat, or wading. The small buildings – some derelict, some still in use – on both sides of the river are fishing shiels, traditionally used to store fishing gear or as accommodation for fishermen.

Most of the fish are now rod-caught, although netting is still practised in a few places – mostly for research purposes, with fish being tagged and released back into the river. While rod fishing was introduced less than 200 years ago, netting is thought to date back to the 12th century. One man would stand on the shore with one rope of the net, while another, in a small boat known as a coble, would pull the net out into the river to form a large semi-circle. The oarsman would then row back into the bank and the net would be pulled ashore.

The path, which later becomes a track, passes the derelict Wilford Shiel and then the Under Greenhill Shiel, part of the Horncliffe beat. The route keeps close to the riverbank until you reach some woodland close to the Hollywell 'pool'. Bear left here, briefly veering away from the water's edge. A narrow path clings precariously to the steep, wooded embankment. It's showing signs of wear and tear on its lower edge, so watch your footing.

Eventually, having crossed the two bridges you crossed earlier in the walk, you'll recross the tiny ladder stile at the far end of the woods. Unless you intend to cut the walk short and return to the starting point, bear right to keep to the riverbank. About 250m beyond the stile, bear left at a faint fork to cross a tributary burn. The riverside path used to continue to the right on the other side of the bridge, but erosion has destroyed it, so you'll need to keep left. After a small gate, walk diagonally across the play area and exit via another small gate.

Turn right along North Lane, quickly following it round to the left. Go right again at a T-junction. Follow

There are several benches along this stretch of the river: opportunities to sit and gaze across to Scotland or just watch the many waterfowl that live on the river.

this lane back down to the River Tweed and turn left to regain the riverside route. When this well-maintained path forks, take either option. ◄

At the base of Ladykirk Bridge, bear right to pass under one of the arches and then keep left to cross a stile. Turn right to walk along the field edge. The path later crosses to the other side of the hedgerow and then proceeds to a lane. Turn left here.

Go right at a T-junction to head into **Norham**. Soon after the Mason's Arms, the road swings up to the right. Just before it does so, take the turning on the left – signposted to the castle. This eventually leads back to the castle's arched entrance.

The first castle at Norham was built in 1121 by the Bishop of Durham, but the most impressive surviving feature – the five-storey **Great Tower** – was constructed in 1422. For many centuries, it defended the ford across the River Tweed and gained the unenviable accolade of being the 'most dangerous place in England'. It was besieged by the Scots on nine occasions, and captured four times. The castle features in *Marmion*, Sir Walter Scott's epic poem about the Battle of Flodden, which took place just 10km south of Norham.

WALK 7
St Cuthbert's Cave and the Kyloe Hills

Start/finish	Small car park at Holburn Grange, about 6km northwest of Belford as the crow flies (NU 050 350)
Distance	15.4km (9½ miles)
Total ascent	321m (1053ft)
Grade	1/2
Walking time	4¼hr
Terrain	Low hills; field paths; forest tracks and trails; damp ground in forest; long section of quiet road
Maps	OS Explorer 340; OS Landranger 75
Transport	None
Facilities	Percy Arms, Chatton, about 7km south; White Swan Inn and Black Bull Inn, Lowick, about 8km north

After visiting the delightful woodland setting of St Cuthbert's Cave, this walk crosses rolling farmland with views out across to the saint's spiritual home, Lindisfarne. It then weaves in and out of a massive area of woodland that stretches on for miles. Sometimes you're striding out under towering conifers; sometimes broad-leaved woods bring a little variety; just occasionally it's more like an arboretum. The route passes the crags of the Kyloe Hills before returning to Holburn Grange via a quiet road and a path along the base of Greensheen Hill.

Leave the car park and turn left along the broad, grassy track. After the gate at the base of **Greensheen Hill**, turn right. The modicum of height gained allows surprisingly good views across to the Cheviot Hills. Ignoring any paths to the left, you reach the edge of St Cuthbert's Cave Woods. Go through the gate and, having followed the broad track for a short while, climb the path on the left to reach **St Cuthbert's Cave**.

St Cuthbert's Cave is said to be one of the many places where the monks of Lindisfarne brought their former bishop's body when the island was threatened by Viking raids. Cuthbert died in AD687 and, between about AD875 and the early 11th century, his body rested in various places, including Chester-le-Street and Ripon, before settling in Durham. In much later times, the area was used as a burial place by the Leather family. It was consecrated in 1936, and memorials are carved into many of the rocks.

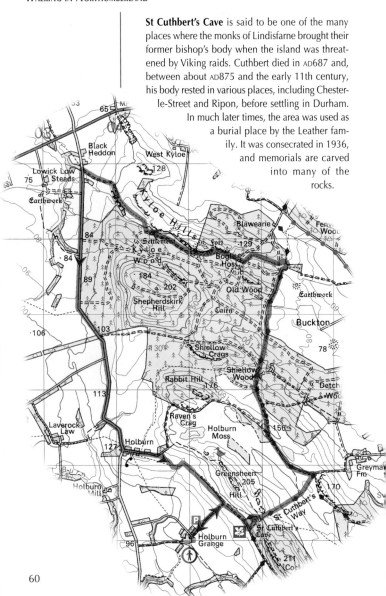

Facing the impressive cave, you'll see a narrow trail climbing to the left of it. Take this and keep left at a faint fork to leave the woods via a step stile. A few strides further on and you'll reach a clear path. Turn right here. Keep right at a faint fork.

Approaching St Cuthbert's Cave

After a gate at the forest corner, turn left through a second gate. The route isn't clear now, but it heads roughly northeast, slowing increasing the distance between the walker and the fence on the right. Make for a gated bridge over Middleton Burn below. Beyond this, aim for a gate on the opposite side of the field. As the faint path swings slightly left and crests a rise, Lindisfarne, briefly spotted from the woodland edge earlier, appears to the northeast.

The small mounds in this area are the remains of **bell pits** used to extract coal for local use in the late 18th and early 19th centuries. There is also evidence that the monks of Lindisfarne may have worked the seams near Holburn as long ago as the 13th century.

Turn left along a stony track. Soon after entering **Shiellow Wood**, turn right at a track junction, signposted Fenwick. The forest here consists mostly of tall conifers, but there are pockets of deciduous woodland too as well as denser plantation. Almost 900m into the woods, the track bends right and you'll see a building ahead. Leave the track here by keeping straight on – along a narrow path through the trees, following both St Cuthbert's Way and St Oswald's Way. Go straight across the next track. A series of bridges and stiles leads walkers out of the woods.

Keep close to the forest fence on your left, enjoying grand views of the coast. The fence and path bend right and then left. Just after a kissing-gate, leave St Cuthbert's Way and St Oswald's Way by crossing the stile on the left. A faint trail now heads deep into the lonely heart of **Kyloe Wood**. It's damp in places, making it hard to spot at times, but it's generally well-waymarked. ◄

In dry weather, it's an absolute delight. Keep your eyes peeled for roe deer.

> In the early 19th century, these **woods** were bought by CJ Leyland, of Haggerston Castle, the man largely to blame for the spread of leylandii. He planted the woods with a wide range of conifers including Douglas fir, western hemlock, monkey puzzle, red cedar, Corsican pine and giant sequoia.

On reaching a rough track close to one of the buildings associated with **Bogle Houses**, cross diagonally left to continue on a damp path. Turn right along the next broad track as it passes beneath the crags of the **Kyloe Hills**. These cliffs are part of the Great Whin Sill, but there are sandstone crags nearby too, popular with climbers.

> Hidden in the undergrowth of the **Kyloe Hills** is an operational base used by the Northumberland Auxiliary Unit in World War Two. The secret, specially trained Auxiliary Units were set up to act as guerrilla fighters in the event of a German invasion.

Having followed the track for 550m, take the signposted path to the right. (This is the second path, but

the only one that is signposted.) Go through a gate on the forest edge and, without a clear path, head roughly north-northwest across wet ground. On reaching dry land, swing left (northwest) along the top edge of Collar Heugh, dropping away to the left. You soon have a fence on the left. (Ignore the stile in it.) Having gone through two gates, join a clearer path heading downhill – with the fence now on your right. This later swings left to reach a minor road.

Turn left. After about 4km, you reach the next settlement, **Holburn**. Take the lane on the left to East Holburn. Keep straight on past the farm buildings. As the track swings left, go through the metal gate on the right. A grassy path keeps close to the boundary fence and hedge on the right for the next 1.2km. The walking is fairly level along the base of Greensheen Hill, enjoying good views of the Cheviot Hills. As the gorse thickens, watch for a gate on the right. Go through this and, retracing your steps from earlier, descend the track to the parking area.

The Cheviot Hills can be seen on the return route

WALK 8
Doddington Moor

Start/finish	Junction of Wooler Golf Course lane and B6525 in Doddington (NT 999 324); park considerately in the village
Distance	7.2km (4½ miles)
Total ascent	207m (679ft)
Grade	2
Walking time	2hr
Terrain	Quiet lanes; farm paths; mostly clear paths on open hill; a few damp areas
Maps	OS Explorer 340; OS Landranger 75
Transport	Bus 464
Facilities	Pubs, cafés and public toilets in nearby Wooler

This small hill to the east of the Cheviot Hills is dotted with prehistoric remains. From Neolithic rock artists to Iron Age tribes who lived in its hillforts, people clearly sought out this area for many thousands of years. Today, the bracken has taken over – but not enough to swamp the archaeology. Take a walk on to the moor and step back in time, visiting rock art sites, a stone circle, hillforts and other ancient settlements. Every lump and bump in the landscape has a story to tell. Even if prehistory isn't your thing, the views across to Wooler and the Cheviots make this short outing very worthwhile.

Take the lane signposted to Wooler Golf Course, climbing northeast from Doddington. Where a track heads up to the right – next to a quarry entrance sign – keep straight ahead through the gate. The dirt track soon dips and then climbs.

Soon after the track levels off – 1.2km beyond the quarry sign – watch for a fingerpost indicating a path to the right. Cross the stile here – signposted Weetwoodhill. The right-of-way heads south-southwest across the middle of the field, but if there are crops in it, it's best to

keep to the field edge. The next stile is close to the top corner of the field. Having crossed it, walk parallel with the fence and tumbledown wall on your left.

Beyond the next stile, you're on access land, although the route continues on rights of way for now. We'll call this 'point A', because there are now a couple of short detours to visit some of the many prehistoric features scattered throughout this ancient landscape. First of all, some of the cup-and-ring-marked rocks for which Northumberland is famous.

Cross the step stile and the ladder stile on your left and then turn left to enter the next field via a cattle grid. Veer half-right (east) diagonally across this field. Aim for an

As the route climbs above Doddington, you're able to look back towards The Cheviot

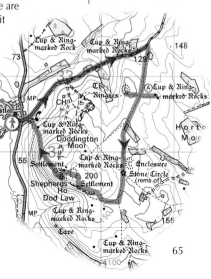

65

The prehistoric artwork here is subtle; little more than a series of dimpled hollows on the surface of the rocks.

intermittent line of exposed rocks on the lip of ground about 220m beyond the cattle grid. ◄

Return to point A and then – for the second detour to visit a hillfort – keep straight ahead, beside the fence on the right. Cross the second stile in the fence and you'll see the earthworks of **The Ringses** up to the right, the site of an Iron Age fort.

Return to point A for a final time and turn right to walk with the wall/fence on your left. The small area of woodland up ahead is called Kitty's Plantation. When you reach it, turn around for another perspective on The Ringses and its prominent western ramparts. Keep close to the plantation edge and then cross a stile next to it. (This is not the stile about 150m west of the trees.)

Part of a prehistoric stone circle

Skirting the edge of **Doddington Moor**, continue with the boundary wall/fence on your left, later crossing another stile. In spring, before the bracken takes hold, the slopes here are dotted with bluebells. As the wall crests a small rise, you draw level with what little remains of an ancient settlement on the eastern side of the wall. A little further on and the trail passes what appears to be a single standing stone. Look a little closer and you'll see recumbent stones dotted about nearby: the site is, in fact, all that remains of a prehistoric stone circle.

Continue in the same direction for another 350m. Nearing a fence, keep to the trail as it swings right. Stay close to the fence until you draw level with a gate in it. Leaving the right-of-way here, but still on access land, bear right (northwest) on a grassy track. Head through a gap in an old wall and fork left to climb the slope. Keep left at subsequent forks to stay on a faint trail along the breezy escarpment edge, enjoying uninterrupted views across to the Cheviot Hills.

Nearing a fence close to **Shepherds House**, head on to the higher ground to your right (north) to locate the trig pillar on **Dod Law** – at 200m the highest point on Doddington Moor. All around, earthworks suggest you're now in the middle of another settlement. Turn left (west) to cross a stile next to a gate. A broad, grassy path leads to a stony track close to a gate on to Wooler Golf Course. Turn left here. There's another hillfort to the right here and a few metres to the left of the path is some more prehistoric rock art.

After just a few metres, as you meet the corner of the wall encircling Shepherds House, bear right along a faint path hugging the edge of the high ground for a little longer. With Doddington visible below, including the remains of a 16th-century bastle house, the path descends. It crosses a fence stile and continues on a worn line downhill. Maintain the same trajectory for now, passing through a gate and then dropping to a waymarker post. Bear slightly left to drop to a step stile to the right of a cottage. Turn left along the lane to return to the B6525, where the walk started.

WALK 9

Bewick Moor

Start/finish	Forestry Commission car park at Hepburn Wood (NU 071 248)
Distance	15.3km (9½ miles)
Total ascent	424m (1390ft)
Grade	3
Walking time	4¾hr
Terrain	Mostly open moorland, but some field paths and road walking; occasionally pathless through heather and bracken; boggy area
Maps	OS Explorer 332 and 340 (both required); OS Landranger 75
Transport	None
Facilities	Tankerville Arms, Eglingham; Percy Arms, Chatton

Bewick Moor forms part of a sprawling area of low moorland to the east of Wooler. Part of it falls within a Site of Special Scientific Interest, designated because of its rich mosaic of upland habitats including heathland, blanket bog and mire that are home to stands of juniper as well as a wide variety of amphibians. Dotted with reminders of the past, it's a moody place that sees relatively few visitors.

This walk meanders across the open moors, visiting atmospheric ruins, passing prehistoric sites and enjoying far-reaching views in all directions. On paper it doesn't look too tough, but a lack of clear paths, patches of thick heather and boggy ground make for slow progress.

Take the track to the right of the Forestry Commission information board. Immediately after a barrier across the track, watch for a trail heading very steeply uphill through the trees on the left. It's badly eroded in its initial stages, making it hard to find, but becomes clearer after just a few metres. Beyond a ladder stile, you'll see a line of crags immediately above. Using a faint trail, aim to

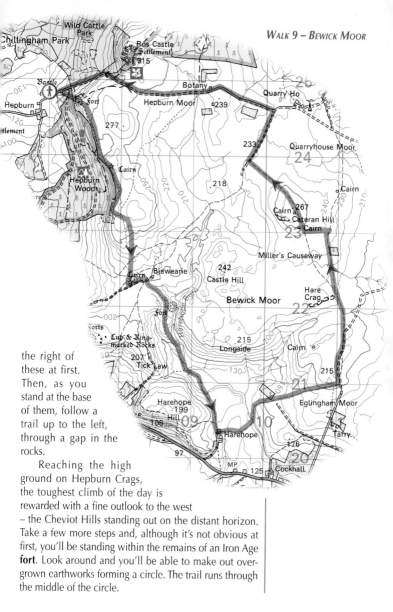

the right of
these at first.
Then, as you
stand at the base
of them, follow a
trail up to the left,
through a gap in the
rocks.

Reaching the high
ground on Hepburn Crags,
the toughest climb of the day is
rewarded with a fine outlook to the west
– the Cheviot Hills standing out on the distant horizon.
Take a few more steps and, although it's not obvious at
first, you'll be standing within the remains of an Iron Age
fort. Look around and you'll be able to make out overgrown earthworks forming a circle. The trail runs through
the middle of the circle.

On Hepburn Crags

Exiting the fort, head over to the trees on the right. There's no obvious path through the heather and bilberry at first, but, when you reach the trees, you'll pick up a trail to the left of the woodland edge. About 800m beyond the fort, a small gate is reached. Don't go through it; instead, keep to the path, even less obvious now, to the left of the fence. After another 150m, the route briefly swings away from the fence, through thick bracken, to climb the slope ahead at an easy angle. It then quickly regains the reassuring fence. With heather waiting to trip up the unwary, there is a temptation to keep your eyes firmly on the ground, but do look up occasionally; it'd be a shame to miss those wonderful views of the Cheviot Hills that appear over the tops of trees from time to time.

Later widening, the path again briefly swings away from the fence. Turn right shortly after this – to return to your trusty companion. Meeting another fence coming in at a right angle from the left, beat your way through the heather up to the left to find a gate in it. Once through this, ignore the faint trail heading south-southeast; strike off southeast through the heather to reach an overgrown track in about 180m. Head south along this, being careful not to lose it when it becomes swamped by high bracken. You'll see the ruins of Blawearie ahead and what appears to be a pile of stones about 300m to the southwest of it. As the track nears the stones, make your way over to them.

> This 'pile of stones' is, in fact a **burial cairn** dating from the early Bronze Age. It was first excavated by Cannon William Greenwell in 1865. It consists of an outer ring of kerb stones surrounding several cists. Archaeologists found pottery, a flint knife, necklaces and burned human remains buried here.

Continue south from the cairn for about 50m to reach a clear track. Turn left along this. In a short while, you'll see a waymarker post to the right of the track. Our route heads off here, but it's worth first making a short detour to the attractive ruins of **Blawearie**, surrounded by trees and crags. The 19th-century house was the home of

The ruined farmhouse of Blawearie

a hill-farming family and then became part of a military training area in World War Two. At the waymarker post, you'll see two tracks – a bridleway (southwest) and a footpath (south). Take the latter.

Keep to the clearest track at all times, ignoring any forks to the left. The route passes to the right of another ancient **fort** and then descends beside the tree-lined ravine of **Harehope Burn**. About 1.3km beyond Blawearie, the track bends sharp left. Leave it here. You now need to head for the small gate about 150m to the south, but you've got some damp ground to cross on the way – as Stock Brook meets Harehope Burn. Head slightly right of the bend in the track to find a faint, wet track that uses boards to cross the soggiest ground.

Once through the gate, bear left along a track. Bear right at an early fork, soon passing to the left of an old pillbox. The track climbs slightly and becomes less clear. Keep close to the fence, and then a wall, on the left. Go through the next gate in the wall and follow a track down towards the farm at **Harehope**. Turn left immediately after the first set of buildings. After a gate,

On Bewick Moor

walk with the fence on your left. After the next gate, continue with the field boundary on your left. Follow this round to the left to reach a bridge over the burn. Cross and go through the gate.

A broad, grassy track runs parallel with the fence on your left at first and then swings up to the right. Bear right when it forks. Drawing level with a conifer plantation to the left, leave the track by heading to the wall on the right. Crossing rough ground with little in the way of a path, follow this steadily uphill on **Eglingham Moor**.

On reaching a broad, stony track, turn left – signposted Quarry House. Leave the track immediately after a cattle grid. The broad, grassy path heading north isn't obvious at first, but if you aim for the clump of trees on the skyline ahead, you should see it. There is some damp ground to negotiate and another track to cross along the way, but, eventually, this bridleway passes to the immediate left of this plantation. It then continues north, narrower now, to a gate in a fence. Turn left here to follow the fence uphill to another gate. (It doesn't matter which side of the fence you're on.) Now turn right to follow the path to the cairn-topped summit of **Cateran Hill** – at 267m, the highest point on Bewick Moor. From the top, the vast expanse of this sprawling moorland is particularly striking: in almost every direction, it seems to head off as far as the eye can see.

A few hundred metres northwest of the highest cairn on Cateran Hill is **Cateran Hole**, a natural cleft in the sandstone that has been enhanced by the creation of stone steps leading down into it. It has been suggested that the cave was used as a smugglers' hideout. The name 'Cateran', which refers to Highland raiders, may support this theory. Local stories tell of the cave stretching on underground for miles.

The path heads down the northwest side of the hill. Reaching a broader track, turn right. This leads to the road, along which you turn left. It's now 3.2km across

Sheep grazing on Bewick Moor

Hepburn Moor back to the car park, which is on your left soon after a cattle grid. On the way, you'll pass beneath the southern slopes of **Ros Castle**, an Iron Age hillfort. You'll also see Hepburn Bastle – a 14th-century tower house modified in the late 16th century – on the other side of the road as you reach the car park.

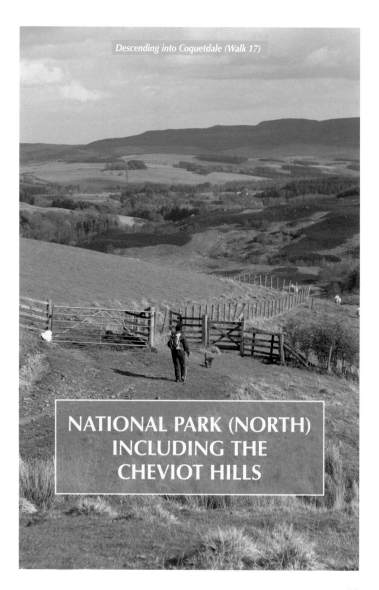

Descending into Coquetdale (Walk 17)

NATIONAL PARK (NORTH) INCLUDING THE CHEVIOT HILLS

WALK 10

Yeavering Bell from Wooler

Start/finish	Free car park at Padgepool Place, Burnhouse Road, Wooler (NT 989 281)
Distance	17.6km (11 miles)
Total ascent	647m (2122ft)
Grade	3/4
Walking time	5½hr
Terrain	Quiet lanes; woodland trails; mostly clear paths on open hill; few damp areas
Maps	OS Explorer OL16; OS Landranger 75
Transport	Buses 266, 267, 464, 470, 473, 710
Facilities	Pubs, cafés and public toilets in Wooler

For relatively little effort, aside from the climb on to Yeavering Bell (361m), this walk acts as a wonderful introduction to the Cheviot Hills. Following the St Cuthbert's Way for several kilometres, it climbs the moorland west of Wooler. Using a series of clear tracks and well waymarked paths with excellent views of The Cheviot, it reaches the hilltop fort of Yeavering Bell, one of the best Iron Age sites in Northumberland. The return route uses a less well-walked, but no less enjoyable path along the northern edge of the Cheviot Hills, enjoying far-reaching views.

Standing on Burnhouse Road with your back to the car park, turn right and then right again along the main road through Wooler. After about 270m, turn right up Ramsey's Lane – signposted Wooler Common. From now and for the next 9km, the route follows the St Cuthbert's Way.

About 650m after joining Ramsey's Lane, which becomes Common Road, take the rough track rising left. Drawing level with a cottage, go through the small gate on the right and immediately bear right at a fork. The path quickly bends left. When it starts climbing, keep to the clearest route. Go straight over at a crossing of ways,

aiming for the conifer plantation ahead. Just a few metres back from a gate leading into the forest, bear left at a fork. This heads up a slope to enter the forest via a smaller gate.

The views north open out on the St Cuthbert's Way

A trail heads through the trees. On the other side of the forest, go through a small gate and continue with a fence on your left. On reaching a waymarker post 150m beyond the forest, turn sharp right – almost back on yourself. The faint trail winds its way back down to the woods. Go through a gate and walk beside a small burn to a minor road. Turn right and immediately left into the parking area. Pick up a surfaced path heading away from the parking area and then, after about 100m, take the waymarked St Cuthbert's Way climbing left through the trees.

After leaving the woods via a gate, keep straight ahead on a clear, grassy path climbing gently. Soon after the next gate, go left along a rough track. As soon as this goes through a gate, fork right to climb beside a fence. Later parting company with the fence, the clear path heads up the eastern and then along the northern slopes of **Coldberry Hill**, passing just to the north of the currick-topped summit. To your right now is the fort on **Humbleton Hill**.

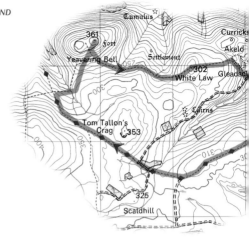

The Cheviot is among the many hills contributing to the scene ahead.

Before long, you leave the confines of the low hills and their many dips and hollows to find yourself striding out under big skies in a more expansive landscape. ◀

The next gate leads on to heather moorland. The path curves around the south side of **Gains Law** and

The hulking mass of The Cheviot

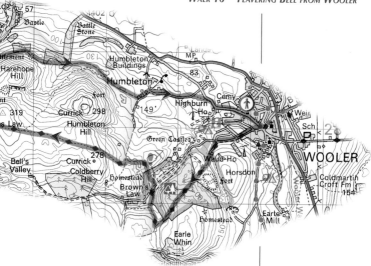

approaches a gate. Don't go through this; instead, keep to the path. Then, in about 80m, bear left at a fingerpost – away from the fence. Eventually, you have a wall on your right. Follow this for about 600m and then leave the track by going through a gate in the wall. The path follows the line of the wall for a little longer – but only until it meets a waymarked crossing of ways. Turn right here.

Crossing damp ground and passing a large cairn along the way, the path weaves its way across to a gate close to the southern corner of a small conifer planta-tion. Once through this, walk with the fence on your right: along a clear track at first but then on grass. The path soon swings away from the fence and climbs to a ladder stile and gate. Beyond these, it heads roughly northwest through the heather – still following St Cuthbert's Way signposts for now. Joining a clear track from the left, walkers are soon treated to some superb views across to Yeavering Bell and some of the other hills along the northern edge of the Northumberland National Park.

The remains of the Iron Age fort on Yeavering Bell

About 180m beyond the next gate and stile, you part company with the St Cuthbert's Way. At this crossing of paths, marked by an unusual fingerpost, turn right for Yeavering Bell and Gleadscleugh. Although narrow, the regularly waymarked path is reasonably clear as it drops to cross a small burn and then climbs **Yeavering Bell**. As you pass through a gap in the rubble of rampart stones that encircle the two tops, the path makes for the eastern summit, the higher of the two.

> The **Iron Age fort** on Yeavering Bell is the largest in the region. The stone ramparts would once have been almost three metres high and just as thick. Explore the site and you'll come across the platforms where 125 timber-built roundhouses were once located, home to members of the Votadini tribe. The name Yeavering means 'hill of the goat' and, even today, there are still feral goats wandering the Cheviot Hills.

Having explored the fort and enjoyed the exceptional outlook it has over the surrounding countryside, return to the gap in the ramparts. Ignoring the path you came up on, bear left and then quickly left again at a waymarked fork. The narrow trail goes over a grassy track and drops to a ladder stile, crossing boggy ground along the way.

Beyond the stile, the trail weaves a lovely route roughly eastward through the northernmost Cheviot Hills. It's slightly less obvious beyond the ladder stile on the 302m summit of **White Law**. It descends east, passing to the left of a sheepfold. On reaching the top of a sudden drop into Glead's Cleugh, the site of another hillfort, bear right at a waymarker. The trail descends bilberry-clad slopes to an idyllic gap in the hills occupied by a single cottage at **Gleadscleugh**.

Cross the stile and turn left along the track. After a gate, turn right along a less obvious track crossing Akeld Burn. Just before a gate, climb the slope on the right. Follow the wall up the hillside – passing through a gate – until it becomes a fence. Now go through the gate on the left and walk beside a wall across the slopes of **Harehope Hill**.

The bridleway comes away from the wall and climbs slightly to pass through the centre of an ancient **settlement**. After a gate and ladder stile, walk east – beside a wall at first. Drop to another gate and then keep close to the wall on the left as you skirt the base of **Humbleton Hill**, the site not only of yet another Iron Age fort, but also of a battle between the English and the Scots in 1402. At the wall corner, turn right. Go through a small gate to continue with the wall on your left again. This soon swings up to the right to join a slightly clearer path and then a track.

At a track junction, go left. Turn right along a surfaced lane. Follow this downhill through **Humbleton**. Turn right at a path beside a bench – signposted Burnhouse Road. Keep to the trail along the field edge and then go through a kissing-gate to pick up a faint track. Leave this as it bends right near a campsite gate. Now bear left, downhill. Turn right along the road. The Padgepool Place car park is 500m on the right.

WALK 11
Great Hetha, the border and Ring Chesters

Start/finish	National Park car park at Hethpool, northern end of College Valley (NT 894 280)
Distance	12.8km (8 miles)
Total ascent	555m (1820ft)
Grade	3/4
Walking time	4½hr
Terrain	Valley lanes; open hill, often on good, grassy paths; paths less distinct and wetter on return route; short forest section
Maps	OS Explorer OL16; OS Landranger 74
Transport	None
Facilities	Pubs, cafés and public toilets in Wooler, more than 12km from start

Stride out along grassy ridges and visit ancient hilltop sites on this rhapsodic ramble through the tranquil border country to the west of the beautiful College Valley. Aside from the initial climb to the Iron Age fort on top of Great Hetha (343m), the gradients make for relatively easy walking in the first part of the day, as do most of the tracks and trails. After a visit to the White Swire border crossing, and some excellent views far into southern Scotland, less well-travelled paths make their way past Eccles Cairn (352m) and towards the Ring Chesters fort (342m). The return to Hethpool uses a well-signposted but apparently little-used 'hillfort trail'.

Walk south along the valley road for 650m and then take the narrow trail rising to the right – signposted Great Hetha. Bear right at a faint fork, making for the fence corner, and then turn sharp right to climb beside the forest edge. As the gradient eases, just beyond the top edge of the plantation, head steeply up **Great Hetha**'s northeast slopes (westsouthwest at first with a brief swing south before continuing southwest to the summit). Storm the ramparts

Looking up College Valley from Great Hetha

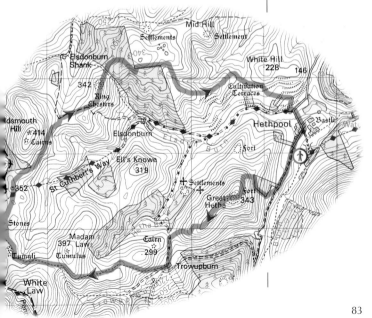

to reach the summit cairn. All the while serenaded by the skylarks, it's hard to resist the urge to linger here, gazing across to the exposed rocks of the Newton Tors and the hillfort on Yeavering Bell, but we have to press on.

> The inner rampart of **Great Hetha** contains nine Iron Age circular hut platforms. At the northeast end of the fort, the rubble foundations are part of a later shelter and animal pen.

Drop west across pathless ground to find a breach in Great Hetha's ramparts and then, about 100m beyond the cairn, bear left along a grassy path. Following a 'hillfort trail', head southwest across the high ground – sometimes on a wide path, sometimes a narrow trail, but don't deviate from the ridge until you reach a waymarker post. Now follow a faint path downhill, continuing southwest for now. About 120m beyond the post, the trail disappears on hitting a clearer path. The permissive route continues straight down the slope, picking up the clear path further on, but it's easier to join the broad route here, following it right and then round to the left. Eventually, it makes its way to a gate and stile to the left of a small group of trees. Continue beyond the stile to reach a surfaced track, along which you turn left.

Reaching the buildings of **Trowupburn**, don't be lured by waymarkers on the gates to the left; instead, head to the gate on the right. Go through this to follow a rough track up a slope and beside a fence. About 150m beyond the farm, bear right at a fork, climbing steadily through stands of bright yellow gorse. Passing to the left of an old stone sheepfold, the path, fainter now, swings west. It later eases its way up the southern flank of **Madam Law** to reach the fence at the aptly-named Wideopen Head. Suddenly, the views ahead open out and you're looking far into southern Scotland. Go through the gate to stride out along a good path (west-northwest). Soon after the ford below Maddie's Well, the path becomes indistinct as it crosses soggy ground; be careful not to miss a bend to the right (north-northwest) here.

Unless you have a burning desire to set foot in Scotland, there's no need to go through the gate at the border. Instead, turn right to follow the wall north. The path slowly comes away from the wall and crosses St Cuthbert's Way. ▶

Keep right at a faint fork, the path passing just to the left of Eccles Cairn, with its far-reaching views into Scotland. Approaching a plantation, bear right along a narrower trail – little more than a sheep trod. This heads northeast, still aiming for the forest. Beyond the eastern corner of the plantation, keep following the fence on the left. At first, there's a fairly broad path, but this later narrows. Make sure you're not lured down the slope; stay more or less parallel with the fence. There's nearly always a faint path on the ground, even through the bracken. Only when you encounter soggy ground, does it briefly disappear... but the fence is still there, guiding you to some old sheepfolds. Turn left through the metal gate on the far side of the short section of wall. Drawing level with a wooden gate in the fence on the left, an old grassy track leads you northeast. Just beyond the top of the rise, bear left to climb towards **Ring Chesters**. The path splits on the way up: the left-hand branch is the more direct.

To cut the walk short by about 1.2km and shave 230m off the total ascent, turn right here and follow St Cuthbert's Way back down to Hethpool.

> The **fort at Ring Chesters**, dating from the early Iron Age, is one of the best-preserved defended settlements in the Cheviot Hills. As at Great Hetha, the inner rampart contains evidence of several stone buildings as well as earlier timber structures. Cultivation terraces to the west were probably used by the settlement's inhabitants.

Descend through the fort's northern ramparts. Follow the narrow trail just to the left of a small knoll and down to a gate and stile at the forest edge. Cross the stile and head northeast along the muddy path through the plantation. About 220m after the waymarked trail swings southeast, turn sharp left to go through a small gate in the wall above – the permissive route now deviating from what is shown on some Ordnance Survey maps. Head east

College Burn sparkles in the sunshine

beside the wall. At the plantation corner, keep straight on (east-southeast) for about 100m to skirt the top of Black Bog. Then swing right (south-southeast), dropping to cross a fence via boardwalk and a stile.

From now until the valley track, although you're on a waymarked trail, the way ahead isn't always obvious; watch carefully for the posts marking the often convoluted route. The next post is on the ridge about 300m to the southeast. On reaching this, turn left along a clear path. At a dip, bear left at a faint fork. The path climbs east-northeast to pass the scant earthwork remains of an ancient homestead. Continuing northeast, bear left at a fork and then bend southeast at the next post. Reaching the forest fence, turn left and then cross a stile next to a gate.

A clear path now heads east-southeast. Soon after joining another path from the left, don't be tempted off to the right. The route is less obvious as it encounters a flat area. Continue southeast for 110m to the next post and then head left (east). After a small bridge, a waymarker suggests turning sharp right to descend rough, path-less ground, but it's easier to bear east-southeast along a faint trail and then turn right along a clear path. This leads down to a track. Turn left and then right at the road. Follow the road round to the right in Hethpool. The car park is now 300m ahead on the left.

WALK 12
The Cheviot

Start/finish	Roadside parking in Harthope Valley, near the sheepfold beside Hawsen Burn (NT 953 225)
Distance	14km (8¾ miles)
Total ascent	660m (2165ft)
Grade	4
Walking time	5¼hr
Terrain	Valley track; rough valley path involving several burn crossings; open grouse moorland, wet and peaty in places
Maps	OS Explorer OL16; OS Landranger 74 and 80 (both required)
Transport	None
Facilities	Pubs, cafés and public toilets in nearby Wooler

At 815m, The Cheviot is the highest point in Northumberland. Its flat, boggy top isn't the most inspiring of summits, but this walk makes up for the hill's shortcomings by climbing through the gorgeous Harthope Valley and then descending along broad ridges that provide great views of the surrounding countryside.

Walk southwest along the valley road. The asphalt ends just before the bridge near **Langleeford**.

> The **farmhouse** at Langleeford dates back to the mid-18th century. Sir Walter Scott spent a holiday here in 1791, describing it as 'the very centre of the Cheviot Hills in one of the wildest and most Romantic sites'.

Don't cross the bridge; instead, go through the gate to continue on a clear track on the north side of the burn – signposted Langleeford Hope and Harthope Linn. This

The Harthope Valley starts to feel increasingly wild and remote

part of the valley is lightly wooded with alder, silver birch, rowan, ash, oak and other native species, but you're still able to enjoy frequent views of the hills on either side of the dale, including the distinctive Hedgehope Hill to the south. Listen for the call of cuckoos in the spring.

On reaching the next set of buildings, at **Langleeford Hope**, the track swings left and immediately right to ford a small tributary of Harthope Burn. A few hundred metres beyond the buildings, watch for a stile in the fence on the left. This provides access to a grassy riverside path. As this heads ever higher into the valley, the surroundings start to feel increasingly wild and remote. Dippers bob up

and down on boulders in the burn, while a few silver birch and rowan cling to the rocky banks. Small pools and waterfalls, such as **Harthope Linn**, add interest and atmosphere. The path is initially easy to follow, but there are places where landslips have left unstable ground. Higher still, the valley narrows, and you'll often have to cross from one side of Harthope Burn to the other.

About 4.7km into the walk, there's a brief moment of uncertainty as the path fades. The main burn seems to be the one to the right, but there's another stream to the

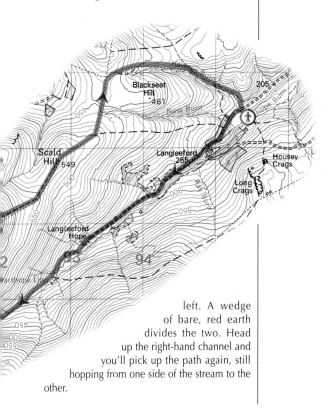

left. A wedge of bare, red earth divides the two. Head up the right-hand channel and you'll pick up the path again, still hopping from one side of the stream to the other.

Emerging from the confines of the gully, you'll reach a fence on the open moorland at **Scotsman's Knowe**. Turn right here. Having climbed to the cairn-cum-shelter on **Cairn Hill**, cross the stile in the fence and turn right along the flagstones of the Pennine Way. Once a notorious bog trot, it's now an easy, 1.2km walk to the top of Northumberland from here.

The trig pillar on the summit of **The Cheviot** is raised above the surrounding sea of peat on a plinth of breeze blocks with a new concrete base (previous pillars have sunk into the mire). The views are impeded by the surrounding peat hags, but as you continue past the trig pillar on the flagstones, the outlook improves. Soon after crossing a ladder stile, the flagstones halt. Continue downhill beside the fence on the left, enjoying views of the Harthope Valley and Hedgehope Hill to the right. ◄

In the distance, the blue line of the North Sea beckons on the horizon.

After a fairly steep descent on an eroded path, your peaty journey continues beside the fence – a reassuring companion over the wet ground, particularly when the cloud comes down. The route climbs slightly to a gate and stile close to the top of **Scald Hill**. Remain true to

Harthope Valley and Hedgehope Hill

the fence as it later drops steeply into a dip where the headwaters of New Burn gather. About 320m after climbing out of the gully, follow the wider path that gradually swings away from the fence. It makes its way towards a waymarker post, beyond which you find yourself on a better track following **Hawsen Burn** downstream (this runs parallel with the right-of-way, which is about 70m to the south of it).

Turn right at the next track junction. Just before the track drops to ford the burn, take the narrow trail on the left. At a crossing of trails just above the road, turn right to drop back to the sheepfold next to Hawsen Burn.

The hills south of Harthope Burn are dotted with small crags

WALK 13

Ancient Ingram

Start/finish	Small National Park car park at Ingram Bridge (NU 017 163)
Distance	10.1km (6¼ miles)
Total ascent	297m (974ft)
Grade	2
Walking time	3¼hr
Terrain	Good tracks; rough grazing; short section of indistinct path through bracken; quick visit to open hilltop
Maps	OS Explorer OL16 and 332 (both required); OS Landranger 81
Transport	None
Facilities	Valley Cottage café and public toilets, Ingram

Take a step back in time on this gently meandering route through a landscape with countless echoes of our prehistoric ancestors. From the tiny settlement of Ingram in the Breamish Valley, it crosses a low ridge to weave its way between hillforts before climbing to the earthwork remains of a settlement on the 303m summit of Wether Hill. This is a great spot from which to soak up the atmosphere of this ancient landscape and simply enjoy the views before returning to Ingram on a lovely track.

Standing at the back of the car park facing the road, take the clear path to the right – signposted to the church. This emerges in the car park of the Valley Cottage café. Turn right to head out along the access lane. When this bends sharp right, go through the gate on the left. Leave this rough track as it bends left near a detached house. Turn right here, along a less well-used track that quickly passes through a gate. Follow the faint track towards the woodland on the hill ahead. Beyond the next gate, it continues in the same direction at first, but then begins a zig-zagging ascent. Keep to the clearest route at all times.

Farmland on the eastern edge of the Northumberland National Park

Crossing the ridge linking East Hill with West Hill, the pleasant track with its far-reaching views descends to **Fawdon**. Go through the gate near the farm buildings and immediately turn right through another gate – signposted Prendwick. A faint track roughly follows the line of the field boundary on the left until it ends at a fence corner. Continue beside the fence.

After the next gate, you lose the guiding field boundary. Continue in exactly the same direction to reach a gate on the far side of this area of rough grazing. Once through this, head slightly right of your previous line

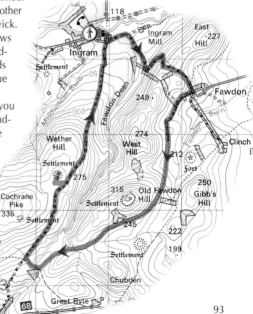

(south-southwest) to climb the slope – making for a stile and gate.

> There are two **hillforts** to the east here: Castle Knowe and, the higher of the two, Gibb's Hill. In fact, this landscape is littered with remains of our prehistoric past – the bracken-covered slopes to the west lead on to Old Fawdon Hill, the site of another Iron Age settlement.

Having climbed the stile, you're now on access land. Turn left, walk beside the fence for about 50m and then battle through the bracken on the right to step up on to a clear track. Continue in the same direction along this. Just before the western edge of a plantation, bear right at a faint fork – along the less obvious route. With views south to the Simonside Hills, this swings around the base of **Old Fawdon Hill**. It later becomes less clear, but keep heading southwest, aiming about 80m to the left of the eastern arm of another conifer plantation. You'll see a wooden hut in a gap between the two arms of the plantation, after which you should aim for the corner of the western arm. The path is about 20m to the left of the plantation, still heading southwest; it's not easy to find, but it'll make progress easier when the bracken's high. Keep left at a faint fork, slowly making for the fence to the left.

Eventually, you'll reach a gate at the edge of access land. Beyond this, continue in the same direction, roughly parallel with a fence down to the right. Go through a gate in front of another small plantation and immediately turn right, through another gate. There's little sign of the bridleway on the ground: it drops into a dip to ford a tiny burn and then heads west-southwest up the grassy slope. Then, after just 250m, you reach a clear track, along which you turn left.

◄ After a gate, you're back on access land, with views of the shapely summit of Old Fawdon Hill to the right. The track climbs gently and passes in and out of a couple of muddy dips as it crosses the streams feeding into Gingling Cleugh. Then, just before starting a more

The next section of easy walking gives you a chance to stride out and take in your surroundings.

general descent, you'll see a wooden marker on the left. For a short detour to the settlement on **Wether Hill** – and a good viewpoint – turn sharp left here, along a grassy track. Follow this for about 100m and then strike off right to climb easily to the remains of the settlement.

Cultivation terraces on Heddon Hill

IRON AGE EARTHWORKS

The earthworks visible today are from the Iron Age and include a hillfort built in about 250BC. However, there is evidence of the site having been used long before this: Neolithic and early Bronze Age pottery was found in a timber-lined burial pit close to the summit. It's a wonderful place to rest and take in the surrounding landscape. To the west are the high Cheviot Hills and, far to the east, you can just about make out the North Sea. But it's the hills closer in that make this landscape so special: the forts to the east that we passed between earlier and the gently rolling uplands to the northwest, dotted with cairns, enclosures and more settlements. The slopes of Heddon Hill to the northeast are particularly interesting, with cultivation terraces, probably created by medieval ploughmen, clearly visible.

From the top of Wether Hill, return to the waymarker post at the junction with the clear track and turn left. This now drops back to Ingram. On reaching a lane near the village hall, turn right and immediately left to re-enter the Valley Cottage car park. Retracing your steps from earlier, take the path on the left to return to where the walk started.

95

WALK 14

Breamish Valley and Salter's Road

Start/finish	Roadside parking at Hartside at the end of the public road through the Breamish Valley (NT 977 162)
Distance	17.6km (11 miles)
Total ascent	584m (1916ft)
Grade	3
Walking time	5hr
Terrain	Mostly clear paths and hill tracks; one short section across rough, pathless ground; surfaced lanes
Maps	OS Explorer OL16; OS Landranger 81 and 80 (both required)
Transport	None
Facilities	Valley Cottage café and public toilets, Ingram

Visit the beautiful Breamish Valley on a warm summer's Sunday and chances are that every inch of green beside the river will be occupied by picnicking families. Take to the hills, however, and the likelihood is that you'll hardly see a soul. This gorgeous walk barely flirts with the high ground and yet the sense of isolation and the views are tremendous. For relatively little effort, you get to visit an ancient settlement, follow an ancient trading route through the hills and return through a little visited but exquisite stretch of the upper Breamish Valley.

From the end of the roadside parking area, take the private road heading roughly southeast towards Little Dod and Alnhammoor. Follow the surfaced lane until it crosses the River Breamish. Just before the farm buildings at **Alnhammoor**, follow the signposted footpath over the stile on your left. On reaching a track in a short while, turn left. This crosses Shank Burn just before it feeds into the Breamish. After a gate, follow the faint path through the wildflower-filled riverside meadows, never straying too far from the Breamish, which is over to the left. ◄

Watch for herons here.

The River Breamish

The path passes through a gate into a small plantation and begins climbing. Emerging from the trees, continue uphill through the bracken. It's not too arduous an ascent; you'll have plenty of opportunities to admire the meandering river far below. Cunyan Crags stand out to the north, a rare rocky prominence in an area of otherwise smooth-sloped, grassy hills.

After a small gate, the grassy path passes through the earthwork remains of the ancient settlement at Prendwick Chesters (**Chesters** on the OS maps) and continues southeast.

Like many others in Northumberland, the defended settlement, or fort, at **Prendwick Chesters** dates from the Iron Age, although there is evidence of Romano-British occupation too. It contains at least seven roundhouses and several later shielings. Excavations in 1861 unearthed pottery, a flint weapon, a glass bead and animal bones.

On reaching a track close to an old farm, turn right. The route now follows this track, generally south over open grazing, for about 3.2km.

About 250m after the next gate the track swings up to the left. As it does so, the bridleway continues just west of south. It's fallen out of use as most walkers keep to the track, but to keep to the right-of-way, bear right along a grassy track at this left bend. On reaching a burn, turn left to follow it upstream. There is no path through this dense vegetation; simply use the burn as a guide until, after about 500m, you reach a waymarker post. Abandoning the line of the burn here, aim slightly east of south for 200m to rejoin the track.

Reaching a gate on **Hart Law**, you look straight across to the Simonside Hills. A few hundred metres beyond this, you'll reach a waymarker post as the track bends left and starts descending more steeply. Turn right here – along a 'restricted byway' known as **Salter's Road**.

On the Salter's Road

98

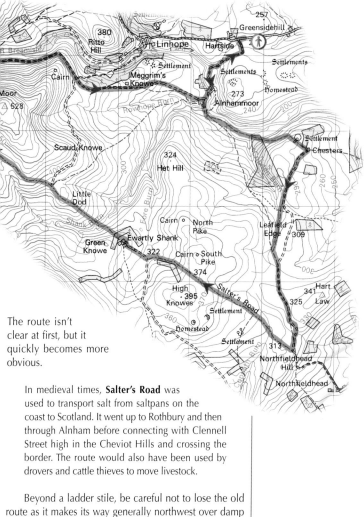

The route isn't clear at first, but it quickly becomes more obvious.

In medieval times, **Salter's Road** was used to transport salt from saltpans on the coast to Scotland. It went up to Rothbury and then through Alnham before connecting with Clennell Street high in the Cheviot Hills and crossing the border. The route would also have been used by drovers and cattle thieves to move livestock.

Beyond a ladder stile, be careful not to lose the old route as it makes its way generally northwest over damp ground. Climbing past a sheepfold, things become more pleasant underfoot. Keep right at a faint fork soon after the fold. Beyond the next gate, the route begins dropping towards the isolated farm at **Ewartly Shank**. It makes its way over to the remnants of an old conifer plantation and follows the edge of this almost all the way to a minor road. On reaching the asphalt, turn right.

The Salter's Road weaves a route through the middle of the buildings at Ewartly Shank, but a permissive route bypasses the steading to the northeast, keeping straight on when the lane bends left. If you opt for the permissive route, it quickly rejoins Salter's Road at a gate in front of a narrow band of woodland. The stony track now drops to cross **Shank Burn** and then climbs. It crosses **Little Dod** and then reaches the highest point on today's route – about 430m – on the southern flanks of **Schill Moor**. The summit plateau of The Cheviot puts in a brief appearance, but it is the upper reaches of the Breamish Valley, visible as the track begins descending, that really capture the attention. Here, swaddled by the enclosing hills, is High Bleakhope, one of Northumberland's remotest farmsteads.

Our route passes through a lovely gap in the hills, following Hope Sike downstream to its rendezvous with the River Breamish. **Low Bleakhope** comes into view too, sitting serenely at the base of the scree and heather-covered slopes of Low Cantle. When you reach the farm, turn right along the surfaced lane.

No one enjoys road walking, but this private lane has to be one of the most gorgeous stretches of asphalt in England. The **River Breamish** has carved a narrow, sylvan gap through the hills, bubbling away merrily beside the lane. The route gains a little height as it comes away from the river. It climbs across Snout End and you're suddenly greeted by a tremendous vista of rolling hills to the east: a scene that'll stop you in your tracks. The lane leads past Alnhammoor and then back up to where the walk started.

WALK 15
Harbottle

Start/finish	Forestry Commission's West Wood car park at Harbottle (NT 926 048)
Distance	6.5km (4 miles)
Total ascent	240m (787ft)
Grade	2
Walking time	2¼hr
Terrain	Road; farm path; moorland track and trails; forest trail
Maps	OS Explorer OL16; OS Landranger 80
Transport	Bus 16
Facilities	Star Inn, Harbottle

This short-but-sweet walk is like Northumberland in miniature: it has a castle, a beautiful river valley, grand views, dense forest, windswept moorland and weird sandstone outcrops. What more could you possibly pack into little more than 6km?

From the car park entrance, turn right along the road. In about 350m, you'll see **Harbottle Castle** car park on your left. If you wish to visit the castle, you'll need to use the gate at the back of the car park and then head across the field to reach the ruins. ▶

This isn't a public right-of-way and there's no access during lambing time.

Henry II ordered the building of a **castle** at Harbottle in about 1157 to defend against the Scots. It saw a lot of action and was repeatedly attacked by Scottish forces, falling to them on several occasions. In 1436

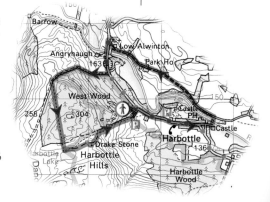

it became the base of the warden of the Middle March, whose job it was to attempt to police a section of the unruly border region.

Continue through **Harbottle** village. Just after the village hall, take the dead-end lane on the left. Keep left at the immediate fork. When the lane bends left, it splits into two paths: take the one on the left which crosses the footbridge over the River Coquet. Turn left along the track – signed Low Alwinton. This passes through woodland and then out across farmland. Having gained some height, you're able to look across to the crag-studded heather moorland on the other side of the valley. We'll be heading over there later in the walk.

A surfaced lane is joined near **Park House**. This drops past some limekilns and brings you back out on to the main valley road at **Low Alwinton**. Turn left and, having walked along the asphalt for 420m, take the second track on the right – signed Harbottle Lake. Ministry of Defence signs warn of the military range ahead, but, even if there is a red flag flying here, you can continue, as the route described doesn't venture on to the range itself. At the top of the rise, as you reach another set of warning signs, you get a glimpse into the heart of the Otterburn Training Area. Even though this spot is only 850m from the road,

Limekilns at Low Alwinton

there's a tremendous sense of remoteness about the vast emptiness of the scene ahead.

The **Otterburn Training Area**, used by the Ministry of Defence since 1911, covers nearly 25,000 hectares. Live ammunition is employed across half of the area, making it the second largest live firing range in the country.

Go through the gate on your left to enter **West Wood** on a soft, sometimes peaty trail. Emerging from the trees on the other side, climb beside the fence on the right. Reaching the brow of the hill, **Harbottle Lake** suddenly appears below. On reaching the edge of this unlikely pool, turn left. About 100m after a stile, bear right at a fork. (The split is easy to miss because the left branch is swamped by heather.) The trail leads up to the fascinating jumble of sandstone boulders surrounding the enormous **Drake Stone**, which is said to have the power to heal sick children. Long scratch lines on some of the rocks were created by the action of ice during the last glacial period.

The descent from this little summit isn't obvious at first. You need to find a small cairn close to the foot of the Drake Stone. With your back to the rock, the trail descends through the heather to the left of the cairn. At a T-junction of paths, turn right to continue your descent. Soon after re-entering the forest, turn right along a track to return to the car park.

WALK 16
Wether Cairn

Start/finish	National Park car park, Alwinton (NT 919 063)
Distance	15.2km (9½ miles)
Total ascent	550m (1804ft)
Grade	3
Walking time	4¾hr
Terrain	Field paths; valley track; grassy hills, occasionally pathless; some tussocky ground; short section on heather moorland
Maps	OS Explorer OL16; OS Landranger 80
Transport	Bus 16
Facilities	Rose and Thistle pub, Alwinton; public toilets in car park

Wether Cairn is a 563m summit lying where the grazed hills meet the heather-covered grouse moorland – a lonely spot with far-reaching views in all directions. Largely making use of quad bike tracks after leaving the valley of the River Alwin, this route approaches the hill from the southwest, where sheep and cattle roam. Passing the impressive Camp Knowe fort, walkers stride out easily across Clennell Hill, Silverton Hill and Gills Law before the going gets a little tougher for the final, pathless pull on to Wether Cairn. The route then drops back to the grassy tops of Puncherton Hill and The Dodd for a gentle return under big skies that, in the spring and summer, are filled with skylarks.

Turn left out of the car park. When the road through Alwinton bends right, bear left across the grass to cross a footbridge. Turn left along the lane – signposted Clennell Street – and then, when the asphalt ends, keep straight ahead on the rising track. ◄

This is Clennell Street, as detailed in Walk 17.

Follow the track for about 450m and then cross the ladder stile next to the gate on your right. Walk with the fence on your right. After the next gate and stile, head east-northeast across this field. Bear slightly right beyond another stile to reach a waymarker post indicating a path dropping left. This leads to the footbridge over the **River Alwin**, close to the entrance to Clennell Hall. Having crossed, turn left along the track.

After 600m of track walking, you lose the fence on the right. Soon after this, but before the track re-crosses the River Alwin, head up the grassy slope on the right. It's a steep climb, but the gradient soon eases as the grassy path passes to the south of the earthworks of the Camp Knowe **fort**. The path then swings up on to **Clennell Hill**. As you ascend, take a minute to turn around; Camp Knowe's ramparts look particularly impressive from this angle.

> The settlement on **Camp Knowe** dates from the Iron Age, although it is apparent from the remains of stone dwellings and dividing walls within the enclosure that later Romano-British people also used the site.

After a gate in a wall, you lose the clear path. Continue in roughly the same direction to climb

Earthworks of the ancient settlement on Camp Knowe

Silverton Hill. From the 385m summit, you get your first glimpse of the North Sea in the distance. Walk north-east across the high ground to a stony track. Turn left along this. Soon after going through a gate, you'll see a waymarker post on the right. Soon after this, the track swings left. As it does so, take the broad, grassy path on the right. This climbs to **Gills Law**, where you bear left at a crossing of tracks. As the track nears a fence, it bends right. Leave it here, by continuing straight on to a gate in the fence. Once through this, follow the narrow trail straight ahead and then, in about 60m, bear right (northeast), losing a little height as the bridleway makes its way down to a ruined sheepfold. Drop to the small burn, but don't cross it; instead, follow the fence uphill (north).

After tussling with the damp, rough ground for about 1.1km, you reach a junction of fences. Bear left here to follow the fence on your right all the way to the trig pillar on **Wether Cairn**, crossing a stile along the way.

Trig pillar on Wether Cairn

The heathery **summit** provides a fine outlook in all directions. As well as the mass of The Cheviot to

the north, you can see right out to the coast. On a clear day, Cross Fell, the highest point on the Pennines, is visible far to the southwest, as are the Lake District fells.

From the summit, return to the stile you crossed on the way up to Wether Cairn and then descend southwest with the fence. The ground on the northern side of the fence makes for easy going, but you'll need to cross to the south side before reaching the forest edge. Having followed the fence for about 600m, you need to swing away from it – before the headwaters of the Allerhope Burn make it tricky. Walk to a small gate in another fence, this one perpendicular to the forest boundary. Once through the gate, head uphill beside the fence. At the top of the initial rise, as one set of quad bike tracks stays with the fence, bear right with another set heading southwest.

Drawing level with the top of Cat Cleugh, bear left at a clear fork. This track soon swings back round to the southwest and leads to a gate in a fence. Once through this, walk beside the fence on your left over **Puncherton Hill**, enjoying superb views across the steep-sided craggy cleft carved by Allerhope Burn and into the heart of Kidland Forest.

> **Kidland Forest**, which dates back to the early 1950s, covers about 2100 hectares of land in the middle of the Cheviot Hills, reaching an altitude of more than 550m above sea level in places. Almost two-thirds of it is owned by the Forestry Commission; the rest is private.

At a meeting of fences, go through the gate and bear half-right with the quad bike track. Bear left at a clear fork to follow the obvious track out over **The Dodd**. Continue down its steep southern ridge to reach the track heading downstream beside the River Alwin. After crossing the cattle grid near the entrance to Clennell Hall, cross the footbridge on the right and retrace your steps from earlier in the walk.

WALK 17

Clennell Street and Usway Burn

Start/finish	National Park car park, Alwinton (NT 919 063)
Distance	21.6km (13½ miles)
Total ascent	790m (2591ft)
Grade	5
Walking time	6¾hr
Terrain	Mostly on good hill tracks; forest road; grassy valley paths; short section of road
Maps	OS Explorer OL16; OS Landranger 80
Transport	Bus 16
Facilities	Rose and Thistle pub, Alwinton; public toilets in car park

From Alwinton in Upper Coquetdale, this long walk heads north into the remote heart of the Cheviot Hills. Tracing the footsteps of cattle drovers along Clennell Street, it heads out across low, grassy hills, past ancient settlements and through forests until it reaches a pretty spot on the Usway Burn. A turning point in more ways than one, this is where we leave the high ground and turn around to follow the burn downstream. Most of the return route passes through the gorgeous valley as it carves its sinuous route through the steep-sided hills. The stirring finale comes as we climb some high ground above the River Coquet for superb views down this iconic Northumberland valley – a grand way to end a grand day.

Turn left out of the car park. When the road through Alwinton bends right, bear left across the grass to cross a footbridge. Turn left along the lane – signposted Clennell Street – and then, when the asphalt ends, keep straight ahead on the rising track. This is **Clennell Street**.

> **Clennell Street**, referred to as the 'great road of Yarnspeth' in medieval documents, is an ancient route that used to be one of the most important routes for drovers moving cattle from Scotland to

markets in England. It crosses the border on the main, windswept ridge of the Cheviot Hills, just northeast of Windy Gyle, at nearly 550m above sea level.

Keep to the clearest path at all times after the stony track goes over to grass. Clennell Street makes for exceptionally easy walking as it ascends these low hills, dotted with the scant remains of ancient settlements. Almost 3km into the walk, you go through a gate just to the east of a plantation. Keep straight ahead, climbing northwest and ignoring any path crossings. At the brow of the hill, swing west-northwest over Uplaw Knowe. Pass to the right of sheep pens and continue west with a fence on the left. After a gate, the path becomes more track-like again. It soon swings away from the fence. Almost immediately, bear right at a fork.

Beyond the next gate, the grassy route of Clennell Street can be seen climbing the slope ahead. Beyond the shed at **Wholehope**, keep close to the wall on the right. The next gate leads on to forestry land. Sadly, the

Clennell Street drops to the Usway Burn

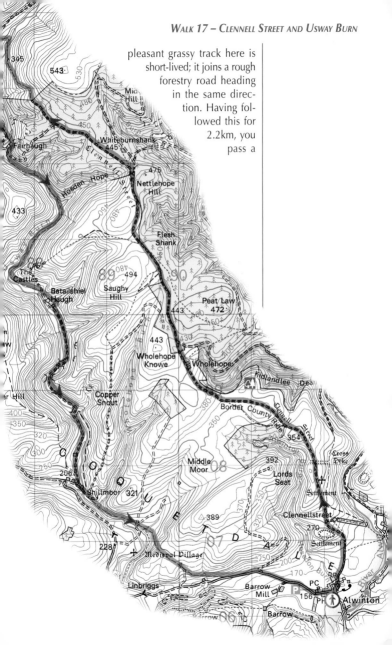

pleasant grassy track here is short-lived; it joins a rough forestry road heading in the same direction. Having followed this for 2.2km, you pass a ladder stile and, almost immediately, bear left at a fork. The forestry road continues for another 1.8km, finally coming to an abrupt end soon after passing a track on the left with a barrier across it. Continue on the muddy path to leave the forest via a gate.

Heading back on to access land, you are suddenly greeted by a view of rolling hills, a heartening sight after the tedious forest. A grassy path swings down into the beautiful valley carved by the Usway Burn. Cross via a wooden bridge just upstream of a small waterfall, a favourite haunt of dippers. Head over to the small gate on the right. Clennell Street goes through this and winds its way up the other side of the valley. After the gate at the top, part company with the old drove road by turning left through another gate. A clear track passes up and over **Middle Hill**, or you can follow the bridleway on the eastern side of this little ridge.

Once over the ladder stile at the southern base of Middle Hill, you re-enter forestry land. At the top of the next rise, keep left at a waymarked fork. Just before the building at **Fairhaugh**, cross back over Usway Burn via a wooden bridge. A trail leads around the back of the building. Turn left along the first track you come to and cross the second one diagonally left to continue on the valley bridleway. Eventually, the forested slopes and felled hillsides give way to more open country. Beyond a perfectly circular sheepfold, a gorgeous section of the valley is entered. The steep slopes on either side add to the strong sense of isolation, but there is no loneliness here; the amiable burn, tumbling along beside you, is a lively companion. In spring and summer, sheep graze the hillsides while skylarks sing overhead. ◀

The good path adds to the pleasure of walking here.

Nearing the buildings at **Batailshiel Haugh** the path passes to the left of some sheep pens. Continue with the wall and then fence on your right. Pass above the buildings and swing left to cross Mid Hope via a small bridge. The clear trail then slowly drops to a track, along which you turn left, still following Usway Burn as it meanders through the hills.

At a T-junction between two sets of farm buildings, turn left and pass in front of the farmhouse at **Shillmoor**. Cross Usway Burn one final time via either ford or footbridge. A couple of hundred metres beyond the ford, at a waymarker post, drop off the track to join the grassy path beside the wall on your right. This bridleway follows the River Coquet downstream.

The walk drops into Coquetdale

Go straight over a series of tracks and then step across Passpeth Sike in a newly planted woodland. Beyond a couple more gates, this ancient routeway, known as Pass Peth, climbs the grassy slopes of Green Side. Don't miss the scene behind you at this point – straight up into the higher reaches of Coquetdale. From the top of the climb, the route ahead isn't as obvious; it heads southeast across the high ground, enjoying views towards the Simonside Hills in the distance. Aim for a small gate just below a farm gate. Once through this, walk beside the fence on your left for a short while. The path and fence then part company as you slowly drop towards the road, looking straight down the broadening valley. Turn left along the road. The car park in Alwinton is 1.3km ahead on the left.

WALK 18
Border Ridge including Windy Gyle

Start/finish	Parking area at Buckham's Bridge, 15km northwest of Alwinton (NT 824 107)
Distance	18.5km (11½ miles)
Total ascent	737m (2417ft)
Grade	5
Walking time	5¾hr
Terrain	Valley trail, rough in places; clear paths on open hill, some with flagstones; pathless section over rough ground; short section on road
Maps	OS Explorer OL16; OS Landranger 80
Transport	None
Facilities	Nearest in Alwinton

This magnificent hill day heads on to the high, windswept ridge that separates England and Scotland. After following a series of burns up to an emergency refuge hut, it follows the Pennine Way northeast along the crest of the high ground. You don't get much remoter than this in England: there's plenty of potential for miles and miles of walking with no one for company but the birds and the occasional feral goat. On a calm summer's day, it's an absolute joy; in winter, a more serious undertaking. Our Border Ridge experience tops out at Russell's Cairn on Windy Gyle (619m) before striding out along a grassy bridleway that gently descends towards Rowhope.

Taking the footpath signposted 'Border Ridge 3 miles', cross the stile next to the metal gate on the northern side of the parking area. A clear, but narrow path heads upstream beside **Buckham's Walls Burn**. Like so many burns in the Cheviot Hills, this one flows through a majestic valley with smooth, rounded slopes on either side. When the burn splits, follow the right-hand branch, known as **Rennies Burn**. The right-of-way is on the west side of the burn, but it's just as easy to keep to the east bank – both options involve rough ground and indistinct paths.

At the next meeting of streams, with a sheepfold at the confluence, follow the right-hand burn again – unnamed on Ordnance Survey maps. On this occasion, it's best to follow the intermittent path on the west bank. Having followed this nameless burn for about 550m, cross it and pick up a narrow path heading gently uphill (east-northeast). You'll see a waymarker post on the hillside ahead. As you climb, the emergency refuge hut at Yearning Saddle appears to the left. You'll reach that in due course – via a slightly roundabout route.

On reaching a post at a crossing of paths, turn left – signed 'Border Ridge'. After the next post, you could head straight up Lamb Hill to reach the border, but our route follows the easy-going, grassy bridleway that swings across its southwest flank to reach the refuge hut.

At the hut, turn right to follow the **Pennine Way** beside the border fence for more than six invigorating kilometres. The first summit reached is **Lamb Hill**, with its trig pillar on the Scottish side of the fence. This is followed by **Beefstand Hill** and **Mozie Law**. The path through the heather is always obvious, and the boggiest sections are covered

On the Border Ridge, looking towards The Schil

with flagstones. The views north are extremely distracting on a clear day, but as you progress along the ridge, it's the hills ahead that command attention: Windy Gyle, The Schil and the massive bulk of The Cheviot. ◀

Watch too for goats hiding in the heather.

The long-horned, primitive British **goats** seen all along the Border Ridge may have been wandering these hills for millennia. Now living totally wild, they are descendants of the goats reared by early Neolithic people, although when they

actually escaped from farms is a matter of debate. There are thought to be between 300 and 500 individuals in Northumberland.

Having dropped from Mozie Law, you reach a gate and fingerpost. Cross straight over The Street to continue on the Pennine Way – signposted Windy Gyle. You briefly part company with the border fence here, but then rejoin it after a short, stiff climb up from Foul Step. Then, on the final pull to the cairn-crowned **Windy Gyle**, the Pennine Way crosses into Scotland via a gate with a National Trail acorn symbol on it.

The substantial Bronze Age cairn on Windy Gyle is known as **Russell's Cairn**. It is named in memory of Lord Francis Russell, who was murdered nearby during a meeting of the wardens of the Marches in 1585.

From the summit, take the flagged path south-south-east to the border fence. Go through the gate and continue in the same direction, gently descending. The path swings left as another joins from the right at a way-marker post. At the next post, marking a fork, bear right, heading south along a broad, grassy ridge. The bridleway eventually sweeps down into the valley. Cross the footbridge and turn right along the valley track, passing the farmhouse at **Trows**.

The bridleway sweeps down into the valley of Trows Burn

Just before the next building, at **Rowhope**, take the footpath signposted to Carlcroft on the right. Unfortunately, there's little sign of a path underfoot for the next 1.5km. Initially, the route climbs a steep bank, goes through a small gate and then aims to the right of the garden wall. After crossing Rowhope Burn, it heads straight up the slope and swings south at a waymarker post. After a gate leading back on to access land, the route continues south for 150m and then swings south-west to a gate in a ridge fence. Go through this and continue southwest. Occasional posts show the way across the rough ground. As you start heading steeply downhill, another post indicates a swing to the northwest – to a gate. Once through this, walk southwest again, steadily losing height. Eventually, you'll drop on to a faint trod contouring the hillside above a dilapidated wall and fenced enclosure. Descend to a broken gate in the fence and follow the now clear path down to a metal gate and a bridge over Carlcroft Burn at **Carlcroft**. Turn left after crossing, left again after the farm shed and then take the access track down to the road. Turn right and walk along the asphalt for 1.7km to return to Buckham's Bridge.

WALK 19

Thrunton Wood

Start/finish	Main parking area at Thrunton Wood (NU 085 097)
Distance	13.4km (8¼ miles)
Total ascent	442m (1450ft)
Grade	2/3
Walking time	4¼hr
Terrain	Forest tracks and paths; clear paths on high ground, badly eroded on ascent and descent, damp and peaty in places
Maps	OS Explorer 332; OS Landranger 81
Transport	None, but bus 710 runs along the A697, 1.9km from start of walk
Facilities	Pubs, cafés and toilets in nearby Rothbury

Open. Airy. Spacious. These aren't words normally associated with a forest walk and yet, even before you've left the confines of the trees, these are the adjectives that spring to mind on this exploration of Thrunton Wood and its lofty crags. The route starts on good forest paths, enjoying spectacular glimpses of the hills to the north as it heads out along the top of the first escarpment. Leaving the trees, you stride out across the open heath of Hard Nab (271m) and then up to Long Crag (319m) and Coe Crags (308m). The crags and extensive views on this second sandstone edge are the stuff of which memories are made: a fitting climax to a magnificent walk.

From the noticeboards at the northern end of the car park, follow the broad track into the trees. After 200m, take the clear path on the right, following Forestry Commission red and green waymarked routes. At the bottom of the slope, as the red trail goes right, swing left with the green route. The woodland here is full of variety, not the sort of monoculture we've come to expect of Forestry Commission plantations. As well as a range of tall, slim conifers swaying in the breeze, there are

Bilberries carpet the ground in part of Thrunton Wood

broad-leaved trees and an under-storey of heather, bilberry and rhododendron.

Keep straight on when the green trail goes left – unless, of course, you can't resist the urge to take advantage of the bench on the right here, with its magnificent outlook to the north. These views come and go as the path continues along the top of **Thrunton Crag**, its slopes plummeting almost 100m vertically down to the lower part of the forest. Keep right when another track goes left.

Go through a gap in a wall close to a large clearing and immediately through the gate on the right. A narrow trail heads northwest through the heather. On reaching the trees along the top of **Callaly Crag**, keep left at a path junction. ◄ Soon after passing the prominent gap of Hob's Nick and yet another great viewpoint, make sure you keep left as the path heads back out into the sunlight.

The gnarled old pines make this a particularly atmospheric section of the woods.

The views northwest start opening out as the path wends its way generally southwest, eventually taking in The Cheviot as well as Hedgehope Hill. Having passed through a gate along the way, you reach the cairn-cum-shelter on **Hard Nab**. The path now veers south-south-east through the heather. Regaining the forest edge, go through the gate to continue between the fence and the trees. The path later crosses back to the other side of the fence via a kissing-gate. It then drops to ford the infant Coe Burn and starts heading uphill. Soon after passing back to the eastern side of the fence, the steep climb to Long Crag begins. The path is badly eroded in places and the bedrock exposed, but the difficulties aren't great.

The top of the climb is marked by a cairn. As well as views of the Cheviot Hills to the northwest, the distinctive ridge of the Simonside Hills now stands out on the skyline to the south. A broad path continues along the top of **Long Crag**. About 650m beyond the trig pillar, swing left, ignoring a path to the right. Bear left at the next fork too, keeping close to the northern edge of the high ground. The weather-carved rocks of **Coe Crags** and the airy situation of this eastern end of the ridge form an impressive finale to the walk's high section. It's with heavy heart that you finally begin dropping back to the forest.

121

Coe Crags form a fitting finale to the high-level section of a great walk

The first part of the descent from Coe Crags is badly eroded, but it's not as steep as the ascent of Long Crag. At the bottom of the first drop, don't be tempted by the faint, muddy trail to the right. At the bottom of the second drop, there's another faint trail straight ahead, but you follow the main path to the left. Don't miss a bend to the right – heading down through the conifers on a bed of pine needles.

Cross the footbridge over Coe Burn and turn right along the forest track. Take the next track on the left, climbing gently. ◄ Go left at a T-junction of tracks. Soon after passing and ignoring a track on the right, turn right at another T-junction. The Forestry Commission's red and green trails are rejoined here. Follow them back to the car park.

This is about 650m beyond the bridge over Coe Burn.

WALK 20
Rothbury Terraces

Start/finish	Cowhaugh car park beside River Coquet, Rothbury (NU 056 014)
Distance	9km (5½ miles)
Total ascent	320m (1050ft)
Grade	1/2
Walking time	3hr
Terrain	Town lanes and alleys; mostly good paths and tracks through woods and on moorland
Maps	OS Explorer 332; OS Landranger 81
Transport	Buses 15, 16, M1 and X14
Facilities	Pubs, cafés and public toilets in Rothbury

Is there another walk in the whole of Northumberland that gives so much for so little effort? This straightforward route takes to the low moorland above Rothbury for some outstanding views up the Coquet Valley to the Cheviots and across to the Simonside Hills. Making use of old carriage drives built for the Armstrongs, of the nearby Cragside Estate, it winds its gentle way through attractive woods and across open moorland. Visit during late summer, when the heather is in bloom and the moorland is a carpet of brilliant purple.

From the Cowhaugh car park, cross the bridge over the River Coquet and take the alley to the left of the toilet block – heading up into the main part of Rothbury. Cross the main road through the town and turn right. Turn left along Brewery Lane after the Queen's Head. Follow the road round to the right and then keep straight on, passing to the left of Addycombe Cottages.

The beautiful terraced homes that make up **Addycombe Cottages** were built in 1873 for retired members of Lord Armstrong's Cragside Estate staff.

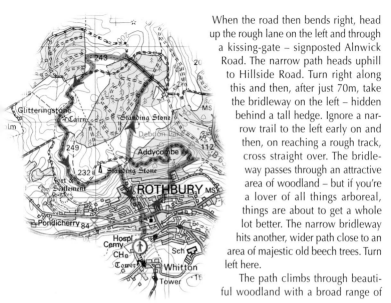

When the road then bends right, head up the rough lane on the left and through a kissing-gate – signposted Alnwick Road. The narrow path heads uphill to Hillside Road. Turn right along this and then, after just 70m, take the bridleway on the left – hidden behind a tall hedge. Ignore a narrow trail to the left early on and then, on reaching a rough track, cross straight over. The bridleway passes through an attractive area of woodland – but if you're a lover of all things arboreal, things are about to get a whole lot better. The narrow bridleway hits another, wider path close to an area of majestic old beech trees. Turn left here.

The path climbs through beautiful woodland with a broad range of

Looking out across Rothbury towards the Simonside Hills

THE CRAGSIDE ESTATE

This path is just one of the 50kms of carriage drives created on the Cragside Estate for Lord Armstrong and his guests to enjoy. A grammar school-educated Newcastle lad and son of a corn merchant, Armstrong made much of his fortune from hydraulic machinery, armaments and naval gunships. He was given a knighthood in 1859 for designing a mobile field gun and surrendering the patent for it to the British government. It went on to be sold to both sides in the American Civil War. In 1887, he was made Baron Armstrong of Cragside, and became the first engineer to enter the House of Lords.

Armstrong was an early proponent of renewable energy, including solar power. He regarded the use of coal as 'wasteful', and his house Cragside was the first in the world to be lit by hydroelectricity. This was in the 1870s, several years before Thomas Edison set up public power stations in New York and London. Since 2014, Cragside has again been using hydroelectricity – with water from one of the lakes Armstrong built on his 700-hectare estate. A short drive from Rothbury, the house and its grounds are now owned by the National Trust and are open to the public.

species, including Scots pine, beech, birch, rowan and hazel. Heather and bilberry form much of the ground cover. ▶

A gate leads on to the open heather moorland. Turn right and immediately take the narrow trail through the heather on the left. In summer, the air here is filled with the sweet smell of the heather's purple flowers. Beyond the heather, the path passes through a gate to enter Primrose Wood. A short section of path leads on to a clear track, along which you turn right. At a T-junction with another forest track, turn left.

You are greeted by three gates at the woodland edge. Go through the middle of these. It continues climbing. Soon after it bends right, watch for a waymarker indicating a path to the left. Take this. It leads on to a little rise of land that is generally overlooked by walkers keeping religiously to the main track, but the views make it well worth the tiny amount of extra effort involved. As the path gently climbs, the Cheviot Hills appear in the distance to the right. Before long, it's the turn of the Simonside

Occasional gaps in the trees on the left provide access to airy sandstone crags and boulders, with stunning views to the Simonside Hills.

Hills – to the left. On a clear day, this is a truly inspiring place to be.

As the path nears a walled area of woodland, it suddenly bends left – away from the wall. Dropping down the southern side of the small rise, it crosses a boardwalk. Beyond a small gate in a wall, turn right along a clear track. With wonderful and often far-reaching views, this track winds its way around the western and southern edge of the moorland.

Rounding a bend, you'll see a **radio mast** straight ahead and a sign to the right warning of overhead lines. Just beside this sign is a narrower trail heading out along the sandstone edge. Take this. It leads to a **cairn** overlooking Rothbury far below.

About 80m beyond the cairn, bear left at a fork, taking the clearer path and staying on the high ground for now. In another 80m though, you'll reach a waymarker post at another trail junction. Turn right here. With bracken encroaching in places, this path drops from the moorland. Keep left at any forks and you'll reach a stile. Cross this and follow the fenced path downhill.

Excellent views can be enjoyed by climbing slightly from the main track

126

This emerges on a lane. Continue downhill. At the next junction, turn right and immediately take the narrow, surfaced path descending left. Go left along the next lane. As soon as the wall on your right ends, turn right to descend another narrow alley between the shops. Reaching Rothbury High Street, cross the main road and turn right. The path leading back to the riverside car park is signposted to the left, passing to the right of the United Reformed Church.

Heather turns the moorland into a carpet of purple

WALK 21
The Simonside Hills

Start/finish	Forestry Commission's Simonside car park (NZ 037 997)
Distance	12.1km (7½ miles)
Total ascent	419m (1375ft)
Grade	2/3
Walking time	3¾hr
Terrain	Forest tracks; moorland paths, including long sections that are paved or pitched; short section on road
Maps	OS Explorer OL42; OS Landranger 81
Transport	None, but nearby Rothbury is served by buses 15, 16, M1 and X14
Facilities	Pubs, cafés and public toilets in nearby Rothbury

The Simonside Hills are the highest point on the 80km curve of sandstone that runs through Northumberland, their distinctive outline visible from many of the routes in this book. Along their northern edge, they form a 5km-long ridge of heather moorland punctuated by weather-sculpted sandstone crags. After starting on forest tracks, this walk covers much of the ridge: from the lesser known but impressive viewpoint of Raven's Heugh in the west through popular Simonside (430m) itself and then on to The Beacon in the east. It also pays a visit to the Lordenshaw hillfort, home to some fascinating cup-and-ring-marked rocks.

Facing the information board in the car park, take the broad path on the right, following the Forestry Commission's red trail for the first 2.4km. Turn right at a junction close to a tall **mast** and then, at the next junction, go left.

Soon after passing a wooden barrier – usually left open – the path crests a slight rise and you can see across a felled area to the Simonside escarpment. The start of the first of three optional 'spurs' – all included within the total walk distance given above – is reached at this point.

This one leads to Little Church Rock, and it's about 300m there and back. Follow a faint, unmarked path on the left. It crosses a flat area before climbing to the unusual rock outcrop in the trees.

Little Church Rock is thought to have been used in the past as a clandestine gathering place, possibly for religious reasons. There are 'cup' marks on the lower, right-hand side of the outcrop – a form of 'rock art', possibly 4000 years old.

From Little Church, return to the main track and turn left. In another 200m, watch for a sign indicating the red route is about to head left. Leaving the track, follow this path uphill. Watch for some interesting markings on an exposed section of rock on the ground in a short while.

The meaning of the **criss-cross grooves** on the bed-rock here is unknown. Some theories suggest this is another form of prehistoric rock art; others suggest the grooves were cut by drovers or other travellers in medieval times to give their animals a better grip on the slippery rock.

Leaving the felled area, the path follows a deep cut through the heather and bracken. At a fork, the red

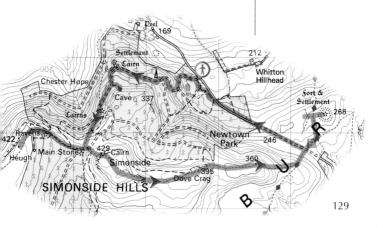

Raven's Heugh is a magnificently airy spot

Forestry Commission route goes left; keep straight on here. A broad track is soon reached, marking the start of the second optional spur. This one is 2.1km long and leads out to the magnificent crags of Ravens Heugh.

Turn right along the track. When it bends left, keep straight on – along a less well-used track. This quickly ends. Follow the higher of the two paths here, keeping to the northernmost edge of another felled area of forest. Just after a gate on the edge of forestry land, ignore the trail through the heather on the right; the right-of-way swings slightly left across the open moorland. Follow it for about 200m – until you see a cairn to the right of the path. Now strike off right through the heather. Before you know it, the ground drops away at your feet and you're standing on the crags of **Ravens Heugh**, looking out over the Coquet Valley to the Cheviot Hills beyond. Those who enjoy airy spots will no doubt want to explore the rocks – at least the ones that haven't become detached from the moorland and stand almost like offshore stacks – but vertigo sufferers will need to keep back from the exposed edge.

Return to the point on the track at which the Ravens Heugh spur began and then keep straight on. The track soon bends left. As it does so, turn right and then take the path climbing left – rejoining the Forestry Commission's red route. A short, steep climb on the pitched path leads to **Simonside**, crowned by a cairn. This is much more popular than Ravens Heugh and yet it's nowhere near as impressive. What is impressive though is the ridge to the east, which we now follow.

Vast, open moors are not unusual in Northumberland, but what makes the **Simonside Hills** stand out from the rest are the sandstone crags that stand proud of the heather. During the last glacial period, this area of Britain would've been covered in thick ice sheets. It was the action of the ice, wearing away the softer surrounding rock, that created these tor-like features.

The flagstone path keeps to the high ground and makes for great walking with superb views, particularly to the north. It passes another rocky outcrop and cairn and then descends through Old Stell Crag.

In summer, look for the bright red berries of **cowberry** in among this fascinating jumble of rocks. Also known as lingonberry, they are edible but are tarter than the more common bilberries found on these moors.

The next top is **Dove Crag**, topped by a burial cairn. On the descent from Dove Crag, you part company with the Forestry Commission's red route, which goes off to the left. Follow the pitched path down to a gate and then continue to the final top on the ridge – The Beacon. This too is topped by an ancient cairn. As you descend the eastern side of The Beacon, the Lordenshaw hillfort is visible to the northeast. ▶

Bear left at a waymarked fork to drop to the road. The third and final 'spur' starts here – 1.6km there and back.

This is probably the best place from which to view the fort's ramparts, although we get up close and personal with them soon.

'Rock art' at Lordenshaw

Walk to the other side of the Lordenshaw car park to pick up a clear path through the grass. Ignore a narrow path to the right at a waymarker, but then take the next, broader path on the left. This leads straight to an excellent example of a prehistoric cup-and-ring-marked rock, covered in several different patterns. On approaching the rock, you'll have seen another broad, grassy path to your right. Take this. It crosses the main path to continue through the heavily vegetated ramparts of the Lordenshaw **fort** and on to the summit.

Lordenshaw is so much more than just a hillfort. Over just a small area, you'll find the Iron Age fort and the field system that's contemporary with it; a Bronze Age cemetery and at least 50 cup-and-ring marked rocks from the same period; two Romano-British farmsteads; and a medieval field system. An archaeologist's dream!

Having explored the summit area, return to the Lordenshaw car park and turn right along the road. Just after a cattle grid, turn left at a Forestry Commission sign and immediately right along a grassy path. This green waymarked trail leads back to the car park.

KIELDER

Kielder Burn from the old viaduct (Walk 25)

133

WALK 22
Tarsetdale Bastles

Start/finish	Parking area at Black Middens Bastle (NY 772 898), 11.6km northwest of Bellingham
Distance	13km (8 miles)
Total ascent	358m (1175ft)
Grade	2
Walking time	4hr
Terrain	Forest tracks, field paths, quiet lanes, woodland trails
Maps	OS Explorer OL16; OS Landranger 80
Transport	None
Facilities	Holly Bush Inn in nearby Greenhaugh

This walk explores Tarsetdale, often a target for bands of reivers coming down from Liddesdale in the 16th century, and visits several of the bastles, or fortified farmhouses, that withstood these bloody raids. You'll also get to see 18th-century limekilns, an old dovecote and, if you're lucky, a wide array of wildlife, including deer, adders, newts, partridges and curlews.

From the parking area, walk northwest along the quiet road. Ignoring a track to the left, follow the surfaced road to the buildings at **Comb**. As the asphalt ends, continue on a rough track into the forest. Take the next turning on the right, heading gently uphill. Having walked this forest road for 2km, turn right along a broad path. At the bottom of the slope, veer right to cross a footbridge over **Black Burn**. Beyond the gate, the track climbs steadily. Stay with it as it bends first to the right and later to the left.

Watch for the Belling Rigg limekilns on the left, dating from the late 18th century.

◄ Immediately after the next gate, turn right and make for **Heathery Hall**. At its gate, follow the boundary wall left and then round to the right. Drawing level with a small gate in the wall, head downhill (south) following a barely discernible dip in the ground. With the wall at the bottom of the field still 70m ahead, come out of the

The Belling Rigg limekilns

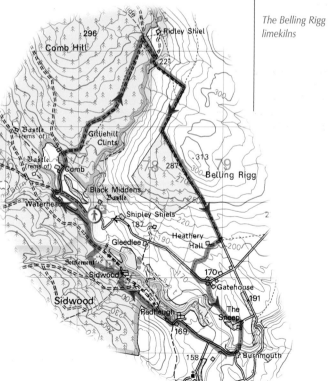

135

The tiny hamlet of Gatehouse

damp dip and veer slightly right (south-southwest) to go through a gate. The route now follows the line of the wall on the left.

Turn left at the road and walk to the dwellings at **Gatehouse**, including two sturdy bastles that have been re-roofed. Immediately after the post box, turn right up a farm track and over a small ladder stile – signposted Sneep Farm and Burnmouth. Follow a muddy track, sticking with it when it soon bends left and then continuing in the same direction when it ends. Go through a gate to walk between two fences and then, when your further progress is halted by another fence, cross the stile in it and continue through the field with a fence on your right. When the fence bends right, keep straight ahead, soon crossing a tiny burn and stile.

With no path on the ground, bear half-left (east-northeast) up the grassy slope and then head to the left of the buildings at Sneep Farm. Cross a stile about 15m to the left of a large gate and then pass around the back of the cattle shed. After a gate, keep straight ahead along a lane beside the farm.

Once through the lane-end gate, follow the line of trees straight ahead to pass through a smaller gate. Follow the narrow trail steeply down through the trees, soon swinging right. After the footbridge over Tarret Burn, bear right to pass between the buildings at **Burnmouth** on your left and the burn on your right. Once over the ladder stile, turn right along the road, soon crossing Tarset Burn.

After 1km of road walking, you have the opportunity to take a five-minute detour to the 18th-century Redheugh Dovecot, signposted from opposite the farm at **Redheugh**.

> **Dovecots** such as this one were built to house pigeons and doves. While their droppings were used as fertiliser in the fields, their meat and eggs provided protein for the farmer and his family during the winter.

A little way beyond Redheugh Farm, a sign indicates you're entering Kielder Forest. There is a tiny parking area on the right soon after this. From here, follow the orange waymarked 'Sidwood Trail' into the trees. Just a few metres into the trees, it bends sharp right, staying more or less parallel with the road for now. On coming out on to the road again, cross over to continue along the well-waymarked Sidwood Trail as it winds through the forest.

Go straight over a wide path and then drop to a broad track close to the cottage at **Sidwood**. Turn left and then, in a few metres, take the Tarset Bastle Trail on the left. Soon after passing to the left of an Iron Age settlement, the trail reaches the steep-sided ravine of Sidwood Cleugh. It bends sharp right here and drops to a track. Cross straight over and follow signs for Black Middens. The trail soon swings left to reach another waymarker at a T-junction of paths close to Tarset Burn. Turn left to cross a small footbridge.

With the burn on your right, follow the trail on a meandering route upstream. It passes the grassy mound of Woodhouse Bastle and, later, the scant remains of Waterhead Bastle. Reaching a track near a cottage at

The well-preserved Black Middens bastle

Waterhead, turn left and cross the Blacklinn Burn via the ford or bridge. Turn right along the next track. At the road, turn right again and the parking area is 550m ahead on the left.

In 1583, a band of 300 border reivers led by **'Kinmont Willie' Armstrong** came thundering into Tarsetdale, stealing hundreds of cattle, sheep and horses, setting fire to 60 homes, killing six people and taking many more prisoner. The bastles that you see in this area today all survived that raid. Black Middens Bastle is probably the best preserved of the lot. The external stairs are still intact, leading to the main door. For defensive reasons, the living area would have been on the first floor, while livestock were kept on the ground floor.

WALK 23
Bull Crag Peninsula

Start/finish	Large car park at Leaplish Waterside Park, Kielder Water (NY 660 877)
Distance	10.1km (6¼ miles)
Total ascent	270m (886ft)
Grade	1
Walking time	3hr
Terrain	Good forest tracks and paths
Maps	OS Explorer OL42; OS Landranger 80
Transport	None
Facilities	The Boat Inn and public toilets at Leaplish Waterside Park

This is the first of three walks sampling the 42km/26-mile Lakeside Way that encircles Kielder Water, the largest artificial lake in northern Europe. Of course, if you fancy a challenge, you could walk it all in one day, but this pleasant stroll is considerably less strenuous. It completes a circuit of the Bull Crag Peninsula, providing several kilometres of waterside walking before cutting across the neck of the peninsula to return to the starting point.

The walk starts by following the exit road from the car park. To find this, stand in the car park facing the water: you will see the Boat Inn down to the right, close to the water's edge. Next to this is another timber building. The exit road is above this. Just a few feet beyond the building, the exit road crosses a tiny burn. Turn left immediately, along the Lakeside Way.

Bear left at a fork – signposted 'Squirrel Hide and Shadow'. A line of grand old beech trees leads uphill towards the squirrel hide. Continue past two small buildings and bear left at the next fork. Dropping to the water's edge, there are two paths to the right: one heading back to the car park, the other keeping close to the reservoir. Take the latter. Go straight over the open area next to the ski

Freya's Cabin

The route up to the right forms part of the return route.

club's building and pick up the path just to the right of the fenced enclosure. Keep left at the next fork. ◄ You'll soon pass an unusual shelter up to the right, Freya's Cabin.

Freya's Cabin was built in 2009 by a pair of architects trading as Studio Weave. Its twin, Robin's Hut, is on the opposite shore. There are dozens of unusual architectural features and art installations scattered throughout Kielder Forest. Others are encountered on walks 24 and 25.

There are few trees along this section of the path, so the views across the reservoir are unhindered, allowing walkers a glimpse into the lonely, boggy hills that straddle the border. After the path passes through a patch of denser forest, you emerge on an asphalt track. Keep straight ahead, and, when this ends, pick up the constructed path on the right – heading back into the trees again.

After rounding The Headland and passing a small inlet, the trail swings right to begin its journey along the southern side of the **Bull Crag Peninsula**. It gains a little height, providing a view into the bay at **Whickhope**. At the next junction of tracks, take the first turning on the left, sticking with the Lakeside Way. At the next fork, bear right – signposted 'Leaplish Waterside Park avoiding Bull Crag Peninsula'. Turn right at a T-junction and take the next track on the left.

As the track begins descending, there are some fantastic views across Kielder Water. Eventually, the track swings left, past Freya's Cabin and back down to the lakeshore path. Turn left here to retrace your steps to the Leaplish Waterside Park. Remember to turn left on re-entering the trees after the ski club. Now, to return via the squirrel hide passed earlier, immediately bear right. Alternatively, simply keep left to follow the main path back to the car park.

Kielder Water with Deadwater Fell in the background

WALK 24

Cat Cairn, Lewis Burn and Lakeside Way (south)

Start/finish	Free car park at the bottom of the track leading up to Kielder Observatory (NY 626 928): the turning is to the west of the road, about 400m south of the turning for Kielder Castle, signposted Kielder Skyspace and Observatory; drive up the track for about 140m and the parking area is on the right just before the barrier
Distance	18.7km (11½ miles)
Total ascent	582m (1910ft)
Grade	3
Walking time	5½hr
Terrain	Good forest tracks and paths
Maps	OS Explorer OL42; OS Landranger 80
Transport	None
Facilities	Angler's Arms pub, Kielder Castle visitor centre café and public toilets in nearby Kielder village

This walk in the sprawling Kielder Forest gives just a hint of the scale of the vast Forestry Commission plantations that straddle the border with Scotland. For the first half, the walk seems to head ever deeper into this remote region: keep a close eye on the walk description and your map and compass to ensure you don't take a wrong turning. The second half is more straightforward, as it joins an old toll road to follow pretty burns downstream through more mixed woodland. The final stretch makes use of another section of the Lakeside Way as it pleasantly winds its way through the woodland just back from the water's edge.

Walk beyond the barrier to follow the rough forest road steadily uphill towards the observatory. Having followed it for about 1.9km, and gone over a crossing of tracks along the way, you'll reach a clear junction. The road to the observatory swings right here, while our route goes left, but it's worth heading up to the right first to visit the '**Skyspace**' installation at **Cat Cairn**, just 100m or so off route.

The Cat Cairn **'Skyspace'** is best visited at dawn or dusk to appreciate changing light conditions. The lighting system within the installation becomes active at these times allowing visitors to 'experience a rich, unforgettable display of tone and colour'. The artist, Californian-born James Turrell, has established other 'Skyspace' sites around the world including in the USA, Israel, Sweden and China.

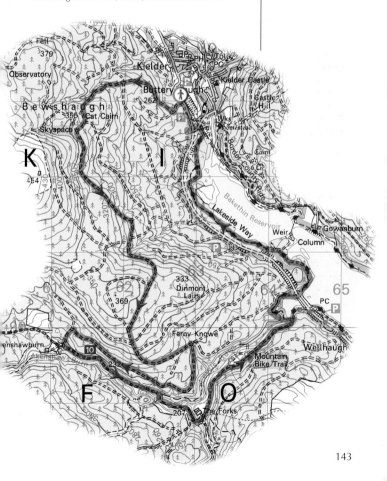

The Cat Cairn 'Skyspace' installation

There's a definite sense now of heading deeper into a forgotten part of the forest: the mountain bikers encountered on earlier tracks have disappeared and dog-walkers rarely venture this far.

Continuing on the main route – to the left of the clear junction – the track climbs slightly and then quickly levels off. On dropping to a T-junction, turn right. In another 275m, the main track swings up to the right. Leave it here by heading along the slightly narrower track to the left – effectively straight on. This heads west-southwest at first, but quickly swings southeast. ◄

With views opening out across the valleys carved out by Akenshaw Burn and Lewis Burn, turn left at the next T-junction. Having descended 1km from this turning, go right at the next junction, along the western side of a stream feeding into Lewis Burn. (Another track heads down the eastern side.)

It's 2.4km to the next junction where you turn left to drop into the valley of Akenshaw Burn. On meeting a broad forest road in the valley bottom – the Bloody Bush Road – turn left.

The **Bloody Bush Road**, also known as the Old Coal Road, was established in the 1820s to transport coal from the Lewisburn Colliery, close to The Forks, to Roxburghshire's textile mills. Where the old road reaches the border, at about 400m above sea level, is an enormous pillar, indicating the tolls in the 1830s. For 'horses employed in leading coals', for example, the fee was 2d each.

The nature of the walk changes now. This is still the heart of the forest, but you now have a couple of lively burns that make interesting companions. The nature of the forest itself gradually changes too, with more deciduous trees lining the route as you head downstream. The Bloody Bush Road eventually crosses a bridge over **Akenshaw Burn**. Joining a track from the right, it then bends left to cross Lewis Burn close to the buildings at **The Forks**. Ignoring a track heading upstream beside Lewis Burn here, keep straight on the clear track.

About 1.9km beyond The Forks, just before Lewis Burn broadens and enters Kielder Water, turn left along a clear trail – signposted for the Lakeside Way. This quickly swings down to cross a graceful, curved suspension bridge across the burn. The Lakeside Way now winds its way through the woods and under a road bridge to begin its journey towards Kielder village.

Suspension bridge over Lewis Burn

On the Lakeside Way (South)

Beyond the bridge, there are uninterrupted views across the reservoir at first, but the trail later comes away from the water's edge. Keep following signs for the Lakeside Way towards Kielder village, ignoring any trail turnings. On reaching a surfaced lane, head left and then, in about 60m, turn right to rejoin the trail on the other side of a barrier. A couple of trails later go off to the right – towards a bird hide. Soon after this, you come to a fingerpost close to another barrier. Turn left here and then go left along a quiet lane. When you reach the main road, turn right. The turning for Kielder Skyspace and Observatory is on the left in 400m. Walk up this to return to the parking area.

WALK 25

Kielder Forest and Lakeside Way (north)

Start/finish	Pay-and-display car park at Kielder Castle (NY 632 937)
Distance	12.1km (7½ miles)
Total ascent	359m (1178ft)
Grade	1/2
Walking time	3¾hr
Terrain	Forest tracks and paths, wet in places
Maps	OS Explorer OL42; OS Landranger 80
Transport	None
Facilities	Angler's Arms pub, Kielder Castle visitor centre café and public toilets in Kielder village

A walk among the towering conifers of the sprawling Kielder Forest is followed by a stroll along the shores of the huge reservoir. The day starts by following a Forestry Commission waymarked route up beside Kielder Burn. Forest tracks, including one that's no longer used by vehicles, then lead through the plantations and down to the northern shores of Kielder Water. Joining another section of the Lakeside Way, the route passes a couple of art installations and crosses the Kielder Viaduct on its way back to Kielder Castle.

From the car park, make your way back down the access lane and head towards the **Kielder Castle** visitor centre. Stand facing the arched entrance and look to your right; you'll see a post with green and red waymarkers on it. Take this trail, quickly going through a gap in the fence on the left to descend some steps. At a T-junction, go left, following the green waymarkers of the 'Duchess Trail'.

Bear right at a fork, following Kielder Burn upstream. Join a broader track from the left. Follow this through a gate and up to a humpback bridge. Having crossed the bridge, ignore the green waymarker to the right; instead, turn left to continue beside the burn. You're now following part of the Duchess Trail in reverse. The clear, well-constructed trail swings away from the water's edge and climbs gently through the tall, elegant conifers. About 650m after crossing Kielder Burn, the trail bends sharp right on approaching the end of a tumbledown wall. Leave the waymarked route on this bend by taking the beaten earth path heading uphill to the left.

On reaching a broad forest track, turn right. A track goes off to the left close to an information panel about the 'Osprey' mountain bike trail, but keep straight on for now. In another 290m though, at the next junction, swing up to the left. At the time of writing, the first part of this track had been churned up by forestry operations. After a few hundred metres, however, it reverts to what looks like a forest track that's fallen out of use and has grassed over, making for much easier walking.

Continue in the same direction after dropping on to a broad track. Occasional glimpses of blue through the trees reveal you're slowly nearing Kielder Water. About 1.1km along this track, another descends right. Ignoring this, continue for another 110m and then, at the top of a small rise, turn right. This linking path soon reaches a well-defined trail

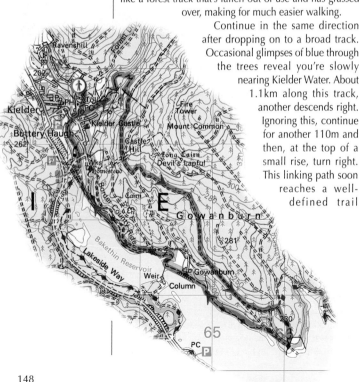

Walking a forest path above Kielder village

– the Lakeside Way. Bear right along this – effectively straight on.

As the Lakeside Way winds its way closer to the reservoir shore, you'll see a cattle grid on the left. A short detour along a potentially muddy path leads down to an art installation: North Viewpoint.

North Viewpoint is a reconstruction, by artist Tania Kovats, of the 'viewpoint' symbol found on Ordnance Survey maps.

Continuing on the Lakeside Way, the route swings right just after the North Viewpoint detour. Keep left at a fork above a small inlet. The next installation, well worth a look, is Silvas Capitalis. ▸

Back on the Lakeside Way, the path briefly goes over to asphalt and forks. Bear left here, staying near the water's edge, then watch for a grassy trail descending left. Follow this towards a lifebuoy ring container and then pick up a broader path following the trackbed of the old Border Counties Railway. Softer underfoot and with less chance of having to dodge cyclists, this is a pleasanter

This giant head, created by a group of American artists called Simparch, is clearly signposted to the left.

Silvas Capitalis, one of many art installations in Kielder Forest

alternative to the Lakeside Way. It later rejoins the more popular path just before crossing the Kielder Viaduct. (If you miss the turning for the railway path, simply keep to the Lakeside Way, making sure you bear left at a clear fork, signposted 'Kielder Village via Kielder Viaduct' and 'Lakeside Way South Shore'.)

Soon after crossing the viaduct, you'll reach a sign-posted T-junction. Turn right here – towards Kielder Village and Castle. Go straight through the parking area and turn left along the surfaced access lane, still follow-ing signs for the village and castle. At the road junction

BORDER COUNTIES RAILWAY

The Border Counties Railway opened in 1862. It ran from near Hexham, followed the River North Tyne to its source near Deadwater and then continued on to Riccarton Junction in the Scottish Borders, where it met the Waverley Line. It had been hoped that it would enable mineral resources in the area to be exploited, but its success was limited. It was used to carry a variety of goods including livestock, coal, stone, timber and beer; and during the 1930s, the seedlings for planting Kielder Forest ended their long journey from Aviemore on the Border Counties Railway. The line was closed to passengers in 1956 and to freight traffic in 1958.

next to the bridge at **Buttery Haugh**, cross over to follow a surfaced path beside Kielder Burn. Reaching another road, turn left and immediately right. Just before drawing level with the entrance to the Angler's Arms pub, take the surfaced path on the right. Then, soon after passing a bridge over the burn, turn left. Retracing your steps from earlier in the day, follow this path uphill and turn right after the gap in the fence to return to Kielder Castle and then the car park.

WALK 26
Deadwater Fell and Peel Fell

Start/finish	Pay-and-display car park at Kielder Castle (NY 632 937)
Distance	20.5km (12¾ miles)
Total ascent	640m (2100ft)
Grade	4/5
Walking time	6hr
Terrain	Forest tracks and paths; open moorland, wet in places; disused railway
Maps	OS Explorer OL42; OS Landranger 80
Transport	None
Facilities	Angler's Arms pub, Kielder Castle visitor centre café and public toilets in Kielder village

This is a walk of many parts. It's a hike through the sprawling forests that straddle the English–Scottish border. It's a valley stroll along the trackbed of a disused railway. But above all, those completing the walk will remember it as having been an opportunity to stride out across high, lonely moorland under big Northumberland skies with marvellous views. It reaches a high point of 602m on Peel Fell.

Head up to the top, right-hand corner of the car park to find an unmarked path heading into the trees. This quickly leads to a T-junction of paths where you turn left. Ignore a faint trail to the right in a short while. Simply keep following the Deadwater walking trail way-markers – a white arrow on a red background – but be careful not to be led astray by the red arrows indicating a mountain bike route. In a short while, the path bends sharp right and ascends beside a wall. Turn left at a broad forest track.

About 370m after passing above the buildings at **Ravenshill**, take the grassy, waymarked path rising to the right. Go left at the next obvious path junction, quickly

passing through a gate and then crossing Lightpipe Sike via a footbridge. After the next gate, bear right along another broad forest track. Turn right at the next track junction. A cattle grid is later crossed, after which the stony way heads out across open heather moorland, climbing steadily. As it swings round to climb the eastern flank of Deadwater Fell, you'll see the air traffic navigation beacon and other **masts** and communications paraphernalia on the summit ahead.

The route leaves the track immediately after crossing a cattle grid, but continue along the track for now to reach the 569m top of **Deadwater Fell** and enjoy the far-reaching views. From the trig pillar, retrace your steps towards the cattle grid. Just before crossing it, drop off the track to the left. There is a faint path, heading east-northeast across often damp moorland. It becomes less obvious as it crosses boggy ground about 100m to the right of a small pool, but a marker post guides the way. The ground is firmer as the faint trail begins climbing, gradually swinging northeast towards the top of **Mid Fell**. The 561m summit is marked by a sprawling **cairn**, incorporating a shelter within it.

Sandstone outcrops line the rim of Peel Fell

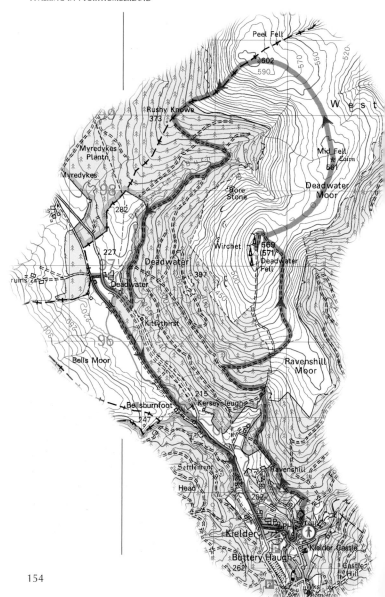

From Mid Fell, the trail, now heading northwest, continues along the broad ridge. It is unclear in places, but as long as you don't stray from the line of short, rusty fenceposts, you shouldn't go wrong. The occasional way-marker provides additional reassurance as you cross this vast and generally featureless terrain. After passing a rock outcrop, cross another flat, boggy area before starting a steady climb to Peel Fell. Still following the fenceposts, the route performs a gradual sweeping curve to the west. On encountering some small peat hags near the top of Peel Fell, watch carefully for a slight bend to the left. Crossing damp, peaty ground along the way, you reach a sign indicating the 'Kielder Stane spur' to the right. Our route, however, continues straight on, following a line of rotten wooden fenceposts to **Peel Fell**'s summit cairn and another amazing 360° view.

From the cairn, continue across the boggy plateau with the wooden fenceposts. Before long, the ground drops away more dramatically. Outcrops of sandstone line the rim of the fell here. ▶ Following the English–Scottish border, the trail descends steeply (southwest).

The most striking outcrop, right beside the trail, is known as Jenny Storie's Stone.

Looking across to the summit of Deadwater Fell

The wooden fenceposts are soon replaced by an old wall that makes its way towards the forest edge. Follow the wall down through a fire-break for about 150m and then turn left at a 'Kielder Stane' waymarker. This trail passes through the trees and then emerges close to a partially grassed-over forest track. Follow this gently downhill, ignoring a track to the right where you head back into the trees. The clear route swings right after crossing **Deadwater Burn**. Keep right at a fork. Eventually, you'll join another track coming down from the left. Follow this to the road, along which you turn right.

Drawing level with the buildings at **Deadwater**, turn left along a stony track. Follow this round to the left, past the former Deadwater Station, now a house. The track, following the line of the Border Counties Railway, leads almost all the way back to Kielder village. After about 2.1km, it passes some buildings at **Bellsburnfoot** and goes through a gate. Continue along a track parallel with the road. On reaching a broad forest road, turn left. When you reach the road, turn right.

After a road bridge on the edge of Kielder village, turn left along Castle Drive. Turn left at the T-junction and then left again towards Kielder Castle. The lane passes the Angler's Arms and heads uphill past the Kielder Castle visitor centre. Ignoring the forest drive on the right, continue uphill, past the public toilets to re-enter the car park.

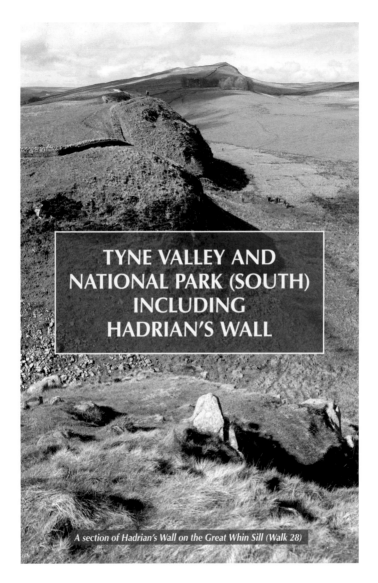

TYNE VALLEY AND NATIONAL PARK (SOUTH) INCLUDING HADRIAN'S WALL

A section of Hadrian's Wall on the Great Whin Sill (Walk 28)

WALK 27
Heavenfield and Wall

Start/finish	Roadside parking beside large cross at Heavenfield on the B6318, about 2.3km (1.4 miles) SE of Chollerford (NY 936 694)
Distance	6.8km (4¼ miles)
Total ascent	156m (512ft)
Grade	1/2
Walking time	2¼hr
Terrain	Field paths; woodland; road sections
Maps	OS Explorer OL43; OS Landranger 87
Transport	Buses AD122 (seasonal), 680, 694 and 882
Facilities	Hadrian Hotel and public toilets in Wall

It's hard to decide what the best feature is on this easy stroll in the delightful, rolling countryside just north of Hexham. Is it the far-reaching and ever-changing views that come from a route that climbs to a high point of about 230m and rarely falls much below 140m? Is it the wonderful mix of woodland, rough pasture and farmland that's covered? Or perhaps it's the sense of history all around – the Roman remains, the Iron Age settlement, the link with St Oswald? Whichever it is, there's no doubting that this route packs a lot into a short distance.

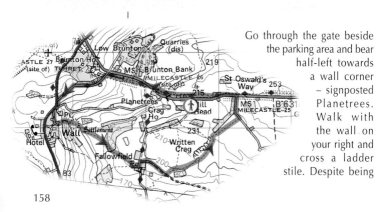

Go through the gate beside the parking area and bear half-left towards a wall corner – signposted Planetrees. Walk with the wall on your right and cross a ladder stile. Despite being on the Hadrian's Wall National Trail, the route ahead isn't obvious: keep to the left of the ditch and cross two tumbledown walls before picking up a narrow trail descending through the trees. Cross a wooden stile in a fence and continue downhill, aiming for a ladder stile in the bottom corner of the field, next to the road. Continue parallel with the B6318. After the next stile, cross the road and descend the steps opposite. Turn sharp right – signposted Brunton.

On the way to the next ladder stile, the path passes a short, isolated section of the Roman wall at **Planetrees**. Beyond the stile, it continues downhill – to the left of a ditch and beside a fence. After the next ladder stile, the trail heads through a narrow patch of woodland. At a minor road, turn left. Turn left along the main road – the A6079. Ignore one lane on the left, but then, just after passing the 30mph sign of the edge of **Wall**, take the next left. As the road swings down to the right, turn left again, passing St George's Church on your right.

Keep straight on between the walls and through a kissing-gate – signposted Fallowfield. After the next gate,

Section of Hadrian's Wall at Planetrees

a set of steps leads up to a third gate. Continue steeply uphill on grass. After passing under some power lines, the faint trail swings slightly right and arrives at a grassy platform dotted with intriguing lumps and bumps – the remains of an Iron Age **settlement**. Keeping to the northern edge of the settlement, you'll pass through a gap in a wall, partly hidden by hedgerow. Bear half-right and cross a wall stile. Now walk with the field boundary on your left, later following it to the left. After a few metres of gentle ascent, bear right along a walled path. Cross the stile and then, emerging from the gorse, swing half-left, making for woods on the other side of the open area. A faint trail leads across the sometimes soggy ground to a wall stile. Enter the woods here and swing right.

From the woodland edge, a patchwork of green fields and rolling hills crowned by trees leads off into the distance, as far as the high moorland of the North Pennines.

◀ Before long, the trail swings away from the wall and over a section of boardwalk before a short climb to another stile. Once over this, head east-southeast – towards the buildings at **Fallowfield**.

It's hard to spot from a distance, but there's a stile in the wall to the right of the farmhouse. Beyond the stile, a trail leads through another patch of woodland. Leaving the trees, turn right and then left along a farm lane. Reaching a quiet country lane, turn left and then take the track on the right – signposted Salmonswell. This goes through a couple of gates. About 200m beyond the second gate – and just before the track starts a gentle descent – go through the gate on the left, close to some waymarkers. Make towards a small group of pines, passing to the left of them after the next gate.

The faint, sometimes muddy track now drops to another gate. Beyond this, turn left to walk beside the fence. The rocky ground to the left in a short while is **Written Crag**.

Written Crag was quarried for stone to build Hadrian's Wall. Its name comes from the Roman graffiti – now in the nearby Chesters Museum – found here by the 19th-century archaeologist John Clayton.

Bear right at a waymarked fork. After the ladder stile, head northeast across pathless ground. Go through a large metal gate and follow the narrow trail straight across the next field. Turn left at a minor road and left again at its junction with the B6318.

After the entrance to the next group of buildings, head on to the grass verge to the right of the road and then go through a kissing-gate into Heavenfield. Walk with the field boundary on your left until you reach the large wooden gate at which the walk started. Before going through the gate to return to your car, turn sharp right – signposted Chollerton – to reach the interesting little hilltop church.

St Oswald's Church is well worth a visit. As well as containing a Roman altar, the outlook from the northern side of the churchyard will take your breath away: Kielder Forest, the Cheviot Hills and Simonside are all visible. Heavenfield is said to be the site of a battle in AD634 in which Oswald defeated the Celtic forces of Cadwallon and came to rule Northumbria. During his eight-year rule, he promoted the spread of Christianity.

From the church, retrace your steps to the large wooden gate where the walk started.

Snowdrops in the churchyard of St Oswald's

WALK 28
Hadrian's Wall and Greenlee Lough

Start/finish	Steel Rigg car park near Once Brewed (NY 751 676)
Distance	12.2km (7½ miles)
Total ascent	356m (1168ft)
Grade	2
Walking time	3¾hr
Terrain	Undulating ridge; open grazing, damp in places; good tracks; quiet lane
Maps	OS Explorer OL43; OS Landranger 87
Transport	Bus AD122 (seasonal)
Facilities	Twice Brewed Inn and The Sill visitor centre with café and public toilets, at nearby Once Brewed

This walk combines one of the most impressive sections of Hadrian's Wall with an excursion into the empty country behind the wall. It follows the route of the Hadrian's Wall National Trail along the top of the dramatic Whin Sill ridge at Steel Rigg before heading north along the Pennine Way. Avoiding the damp ground beside Greenlee Lough, it gains a little height to return to the Steel Rigg car park via a series of grassy paths and stony tracks.

Walk to the far end of the car park and take the path on the right. Follow it round to the left, through a gate. When the constructed path ends, follow the line of the wall down to the right to pick up a paved path. Head left along this to climb up the side of Peel Crags. At the top of the short but steep ascent, the path passes through a wall gap and a kissing-gate before heading left.

This is a much-photographed section of Hadrian's Wall, the turf-topped remains of the Roman fortification snaking its way along the crest of the Great Whin Sill, the dolerite rock that forms this distinctive, undulating ridge. Religiously

Hotbank farm with Crag Lough behind

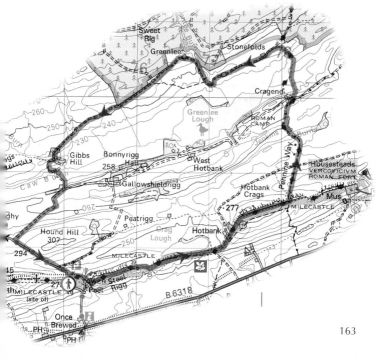

163

following the lie of the land, the wall path soars and plummets repeatedly – hard-going for anyone attempting a long section along the National Trail. You'll see the remains of **Milecastle 39** in one of these many dips.

> **Milecastles** were small forts placed at intervals of approximately one Roman mile all along Hadrian's Wall, and there would have been two turrets – small watch towers – between milecastles. The next trough on the ridge may seem familiar to film fans – known as Sycamore Gap, it featured in the 1991 blockbuster *Robin Hood: Prince of Thieves* starring Kevin Costner.

The path stays a reasonably safe distance from the edge, but it's hard to resist inching closer to the vertiginous abyss to look down on the water below.

Crossing to the other side of the wall again just after Sycamore Gap, you climb to the top of the steep and spectacular crags fringing the south side of **Crag Lough**. ◄

Soon after passing through an attractive stand of pines, cross a farm track and go through the small gate opposite – signposted Housesteads. Passing to the right of the farm at **Hotbank**, the route climbs again. Keep close to the wall on the left. If you're here at a quiet time, there's a wonderful sense of isolation about this stretch of Hadrian's Wall: the land on both sides is sparsely populated. To the north, in fact, there's little but scattered farmsteads, rough grazing and the border forests.

Part company with the Hadrian's Wall Path at the next dip on the ridge. Cross the ladder stile next to the gate on the left to continue on the **Pennine Way** – signposted Leadgate. After just a few strides, bear right along a grassy trail cutting diagonally across this parcel of rough grazing. Cross a ladder stile next to a metal gate. Resisting the lure of the solid track straight ahead, bear left (north-northeast) along a muddier track. After the next gate/ladder stile, a pleasanter track winds its way across the open ground. Beyond another gate, cross a muddy track and swing right, following the acorn waymarkers of the National Trail. The track quickly bends left and you'll see **Greenlee Lough** ahead.

A national nature reserve, **Greenlee Lough** is the largest natural lake in Northumberland. In winter, the wetland hosts migratory species such as Whooper swans, goldeneye, goosander, pochard, wigeon, teal and a range of geese including greylag, pink-footed and barnacle. Osprey visit in the summer and the lake is also home to otters, the rare native white-clawed crayfish and unusual water-loving plants such as bogbean and marsh cinquefoil. The bogs and heath are an ideal breeding ground for the large heath butterfly, while buntings and warblers thrive in the reeds and woods.

The Roman wall undulates with the dolerite ridge

About 110m beyond the next bend to the right, watch carefully for a waymarker post up to the right. It's easy to lose sight of the path here, but the waymarkers are a reliable guide. They eventually lead to a ladder stile about 260m east of the farm at East Stonefolds. Cross this and, leaving the Pennine Way, turn left – signposted Greenlee.

A track passes to the left of the farmhouse and continues to West Stonefolds. Go through the yard, leaving the garden via a gate/stile. Turn left, walking beside a

Near Greenlee Lough, the largest natural lake in Northumberland

wall. At the wall corner, swing down to the footbridge over **Greenlee Burn**. After a ladder stile, follow the fence up to a step stile. Continue straight on to reach a finger-post next to a gate on the left. Now head up the grassy slope on the right towards the farm at **Greenlee**.

Beyond the next gate/stile, join a clearer path. With good views of Greenlee Lough, follow this to the left of the farmhouse and then to a gate. Once through this, bear left along a stony track. After the muddy Pennine Way, this makes for easy walking: a chance to stride out and really enjoy the lonely country 'beyond the wall'. Eventually, nearing a farm shed, the track swings right. At the entrance to **Gibbs Hill** Farm, cross the road bridge on the right and follow the surfaced lane up to a T-junction. Go left here. The car park where the walk started is on the left in about 850m.

WALK 29
Vindolanda and Crag Lough

Start/finish	Steel Rigg car park near Once Brewed (NY 751 676)
Distance	8.5km (5¼ miles)
Total ascent	218m (715ft)
Grade	1/2
Walking time	2½hr
Terrain	Quiet lanes; farm paths; rough pasture, wet in places
Maps	OS Explorer OL43; OS Landranger 86
Transport	Bus AD122 (seasonal)
Facilities	Twice Brewed Inn and The Sill visitor centre with café and public toilets, at Once Brewed

This route heads into Hadrian's Wall country to experience both the Roman-controlled side of the once mighty empire's border and the wild lands to the north. It passes the massive archaeological site and museum at Vindolanda, well worth a visit if time allows. (Admission fees apply.) Passing a well-preserved Roman milestone along the way, it then climbs to the route of Hadrian's Wall. With impressive views of the craggy Whin Sill ridge on which the ancient structure sits, it crosses the large meadows and open pasture where, come spring, curlews return to nest.

From the entrance to the Steel Rigg car park, turn left along the quiet road. Before losing height, you're able to look straight across the Tyne valley to the open moorland of the North Pennines.

On reaching the B6318 at **Once Brewed**, cross diagonally right to walk down the road signposted to Vindolanda. ▶ Take the next road on the left, still following signs for Vindolanda. The thatched building on the left about half-way along this road is **Causeway House**.

The new building on the right is the The Sill, Northumberland National Park's £14.8m visitor centre.

Built in 1770, **Causeway House** is a former farm-house and the only building in Northumberland

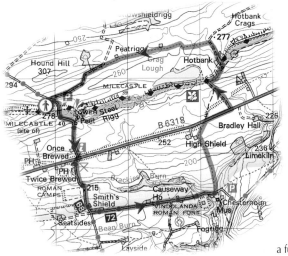

still thatched with heather, a roof covering known locally as black thack.

You'll see **Vindolanda**'s car park on the right about 1.2km along this road. Unless you're calling in at the site, continue on the now narrower lane. In a further 500m, watch for a ladder stile on the left (opposite the entrance to Codley Gate). Cross the stile – signposted High Shield. You'll see the **Chesterholm** Roman milestone on the left here, located on the Stanegate.

Follow the muddy track away from the wall. It quickly ends. When it does, continue north-northwest. At the top of the first rise, take a moment to look back: from

The substantial Roman remains at Vindolanda

VINDOLANDA

The fort at Vindolanda was built before Hadrian's Wall to guard the Stanegate, the Roman road linking Corbridge and Carlisle. The site was purchased in the 1930s by archaeologist Eric Birley and is a work in progress, his descendants continuing the dig that he began all those decades ago.

The site of the unearthed fort is vast and many impressive discoveries have been made over the years, including wooden writing tablets dating from AD92. When these were first discovered in 1973, they were the oldest handwritten documents ever to be found in Britain. (In 2010, tablets dating from AD50-80 were found during a dig in central London.) The Vindolanda tablets contain official military records as well as personal matters, including an invitation to an AD100 birthday party. Another uses the term 'Brittunculi', or 'wretched little Britons' to describe the indigenous population. So far, more than 700 tablets have been transcribed and translated. Most are kept in the British Museum, although a small number are on display at Vindolanda.

Visit www.vindolanda.com for more details and information on admission prices and opening times.

here, there's a good sense of the scale of Vindolanda. Drift towards the fence on the right and follow it uphill towards the buildings at **High Shield**. After a ladder stile close to the buildings, you quickly join a muddy track. Follow this for about 50m and then cross the stile to the right. Head northeast across the field.

> Straight ahead, on the other side of the B6318, are some parallel mounds with a ditch between them. This is the **vallum**, built just to the south of Hadrian's Wall. Its exact purpose has been the cause of much debate over the years, but it's now generally thought to mark the southern edge of the Roman military zone.

Turn right along the B6318 for about 360m and then take the gated farm track on the left. Leave this track at the point at which is crosses the Hadrian's Wall Path. Go through the gate on the right here to follow the National Trail towards Housesteads. As the path draws level with

The lonely country north of the Roman wall

the farm at **Hotbank**, turn left through the gate. Join a track passing to the right of the farm buildings and follow it out through a metal gate. The track crosses an area of enclosed pasture behind the farm. From here, there's a good view of **Crag Lough** and the dark cliffs towering over it. When the track forks, keep right. After a ladder stile, turn left.

As indicated by the sign, please walk in single file here.

Beyond a step stile, a faint, sometimes wet path crosses two hay meadows (west-southwest). ◄ On the far side of the second meadow, on reaching a fingerpost, swing right along a faint track leading to a ladder stile. Beyond this, resume your west-southwest line. You'll quickly reach a wall corner. From here, walk with the wall on your immediate right.

All the while, the crags of the Great Whin Sill form a formidable barrier to the south. From our path, it's clear why Hadrian chose to build his wall along the top of this impressive ridge. During the summer, the ridge is often lined with walkers: some doing the Hadrian's Wall Path, some walking the Pennine Way, others just out for the day. But here, in the wilds beyond the wall, you're likely to have the path to yourself, accompanied only by the bleating of the sheep and the calls, in spring and early summer, of nesting curlews.

Soon after a ladder stile, the path becomes more track-like. This is followed all the way to a minor lane. Turn left and the car park is on the left in 170m.

WALK 30

Best of Hadrian's Wall

Start	Car park at Walltown Crags near Greenhead (NY 668 659)
Finish	Car park at Housesteads Fort (NY 792 683)
Distance	13.9km (8½ miles)
Total ascent	507m (1663ft)
Grade	3
Walking time	5hr
Terrain	Undulating ridge
Maps	OS Explorer OL43; OS Landranger 86 and 87 (both required)
Transport	The start and finish points are linked by bus AD122 (seasonal)
Facilities	Café at Roman Army Museum (Walltown); snacks, hot drinks and public toilets in Walltown Crags car park; refreshments and public toilets at Housesteads Fort car park

This walk tackles the most scenically impressive and physically challenging sections of the Hadrian's Wall Path in one go. For nearly 14 amazing kilometres, from Walltown Crags in the west to Housesteads Fort in the east, the Roman Wall runs along the apex of the roller-coaster Great Whin Sill, a ridge of dolerite formed by a magma flow about 300 million years ago. The combination of this impressive natural feature and the enduring man-made structure, stretching ahead into the distance, makes this a truly stunning walk. Allow plenty of time for all the ups and downs – as well as countless photo opportunities.

Heading away from the car park entrance, take the track beside the small building housing a tiny café and toilets. Keep left, following the acorn symbols indicating the route of the Hadrian's Wall Path and Pennine Way. As you climb away from the old quarry, go through a gate and turn left to ascend gently beside a wall on your left. On nearing Hadrian's Wall, swing right, quickly reaching the top of the ridge. To the north are the lonely commons and forests that straddle the English–Scottish border.

Soon after passing above a farm, the route drops into a dip where an ordinary farm wall is crossed via a ladder stile. This is the first of many such depressions along the ridge, created by meltwater at the end of the last glacial period. Just after an area of woodland, you pass in front of an isolated farmhouse and continue in roughly the same

Milecastle on Hadrian's Wall

map continues
on page 174

direction with a drystone wall on your left. Successions of the dolerite ridge can be seen beyond the next group of buildings at Great Chesters, each one higher than the one before, promising tough walking ahead.

The field in front of the farm at **Great Chesters** contains the remains of **Aesica Roman Fort**. The route passes next to it. On reaching a narrow lane, go right, cross a bridge over a small burn and then turn left. Go through the gate on your right to enter the **Cawfields** car park and immediately turn left – signposted Steel Rigg. A clear path runs along the edge of the quarry pool.

After a kissing-gate, the trail swings right and climbs, via another gate, to a gap in Hadrian's Wall. Go through this and turn left to continue beside the Roman remains. Almost immediately, you pass **Milecastle 42**. A delightfully undulating path continues east beside the wall, still following the top of the Great Whin Sill. Soon after passing Caw Gap **Turret**, the wall and its associated path drop to a minor road. Cross straight over to continue along the wall path. Passing **Milecastle 41** along the way, you ascend to the **trig point** on Winshields Crag. ▶

At 345m, this is the highest point on the entire wall.

The next road is crossed close to the Steel Riggs car park. Cross over to join a constructed path, now on the north side of the wall. The walk now coincides with the start of Walk 28, where full details of features along this section can be found. Soon after a gate, the surfaced path ends. Follow the line of the wall down to the right to pick up a paved path. Head left along this to climb up the side

Walkers on the Hadrian's Wall Path

of Peel Crags. At the top of the short but steep ascent, the path passes through a wall gap and a kissing-gate before heading left. Crossing to the other side of the wall again just after Sycamore Gap, you climb to the top of the steep and spectacular crags fringing the south side of **Crag Lough**.

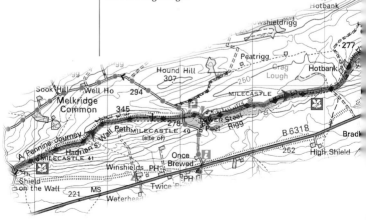

Soon after passing through an attractive stand of pines, cross a farm track and go through the small gate opposite – signposted Housesteads. Passing to the right of the farm at **Hotbank**, the route climbs again. Keep close to the wall on the left as you make your way uphill. About 3.9km beyond the Hotbank track, you near a small area of woodland. Just before reaching the gate leading into the trees, swing right, dropping to a gate and ladder stile just below the woods. Walk parallel with the woodland edge above, crossing one more stile on your way to the walls of **Housesteads (Vercovicium) Roman Fort**.

> **Housesteads (Vercovicium) Fort** housed up to 1000 auxiliary infantry. Most of the remains that can be seen today, including four double gateways and stone ramparts that are a metre-and-a-half thick, date from the third and fourth centuries.

Drop right to reach a group of surfaced paths close to the **museum**. The higher one on the left leads to the fort's south entrance. You want the path below this, heading downhill to the visitor centre, car park and bus stop for the AD122 seasonal bus service back to Walltown Crags.

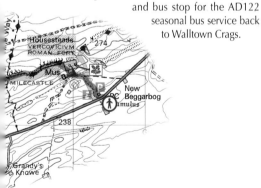

WALK 31

Haltwhistle and the South Tyne

Start/finish	Haltwhistle Railway Station (NY 704 637)
Distance	15.6km (9¾ miles)
Total ascent	290m (950ft)
Grade	2
Walking time	4hr
Terrain	Disused railway (surfaced); quiet roads; riverside track; woodland trail; farm paths
Maps	OS Explorer OL43; OS Landranger 86
Transport	Haltwhistle is on the Carlisle-Newcastle railway line and is served by buses AD122 (seasonal), 685, 185, 681 and X122
Facilities	Pubs, cafés and public toilets in Haltwhistle; Wallace Arms at Rowfoot, Featherstone

The River South Tyne rises in the North Pennines and then flows north to Haltwhistle before heading east to team up with the River North Tyne near Hexham. Starting from the small town of Haltwhistle, said to be the geographical centre of Britain, this walk explores the river valley as it emerges from the confines of the hills. It starts by following the South Tyne Trail along a disused railway through the middle of rough pastureland and in and out of pretty woodland. After crossing the impressive Lambley Viaduct, the route heads back downstream via field paths and woodland trails.

From the platform on the northern side of Haltwhistle Station, cross the pedestrian bridge and then head left from the Carlisle-bound platform. Dropping to the right of the signal box, you come out at the end of a bridge over the River South Tyne.

Ignoring the bridge, keep straight on and, immediately after some information panels, take the path rising left. This comes out on the viaduct known as the Alston Arches as it crosses the River South Tyne, the first of many

crossings on this walk. Look west from the
viaduct and you'll see the northernmost hills of the Pennines. On
the south bank, the path
swings right. When
you see a panel
with wildlife

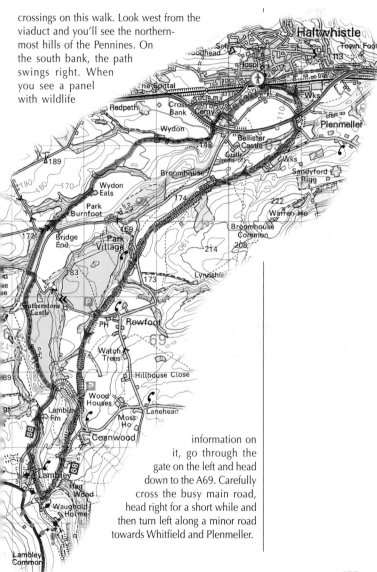

information on
it, go through the
gate on the left and head
down to the A69. Carefully
cross the busy main road,
head right for a short while and
then turn left along a minor road
towards Whitfield and Plenmeller.

River South Tyne

There is a pedestrian path to the left of the asphalt. When this ends, cross over and head through the gap opposite to join a surfaced cycle route.

This is part of the **South Tyne Trail**, a 37km route linking Haltwhistle with the source of the river near Garrigill. At this stage, the South Tyne Trail follows the trackbed of the former Alston to Haltwhistle branch line. This was constructed mainly to serve the lead and coal mines around Alston. It opened in 1852 and finally closed to passengers in 1976.

Having followed the surfaced path for 2.8km, you reach a minor road near **Park Village**. Cross diagonally left to continue on the South Tyne Trail. Other roads are crossed immediately after the old station at Featherstone Park, with its lovely grass-covered platform, and then just beyond the parking bays beside the trail at **Coanwood**.

After the disused platform at the former Coanwood Station, don't be tempted by the path to the right. Keep to the higher path and cross Lambley Viaduct, with its superb views of the river 32m below. At the far end,

descend the steps on the right. Reaching a path junction, climb the steps on the left – signposted Lambley. Don't go through the small gate just beyond the steps; instead, turn right along a path running along the upper edge of the river's steep, wooded embankment. This later bends left to emerge on a minor road through the tranquil hamlet of **Lambley**. Turn right here and right again at a T-junction.

View north from Lambley Viaduct

Having crossed back over the South Tyne – on a road bridge this time – take the path signposted to Featherstone on the left. This goes through a pedestrian gate beside a larger farm gate. A riverside track is now followed downstream for about 1.6km. Make sure you keep close to the river as you pass the remains of a prisoner-of-war camp.

'CAMP 18'

The camp near Featherstone Castle was built in 1944 to accommodate American soldiers preparing for the D-Day landings. Known as 'Camp 18', it was then used to house Italian prisoners of war before becoming a temporary home to several thousand German officers until it was closed in 1948.

PoWs were graded into three main ideological groups – white, grey and black. Camp 18 housed 'black' prisoners, the most hard-line Nazis who were regarded as requiring 're-education' before they could be repatriated to Germany after the war. The camp had its own theatre, library, chapel and medical centre. It had a newspaper, *Die Zeit am Tyne*, printed in Hexham, and PoWs received visiting lecturers from top British universities.

The most senior German to be held at Camp 18 was General Ferdinand Heim, who was Chief of Staff to the Sixth Army. Following the Battle of Stalingrad, in which the Germans suffered a humiliating defeat, he was dismissed from the army. Reinstated in 1944, he was sent to Boulogne in France, where he and his men eventually surrendered to Canadian soldiers.

At the northern end of the track, close to **Featherstone Castle**, bear left to walk on a strip of land beside the river on your left and a fence on your right. Cross the footbridge – signposted Kellah. Ignoring steps on the west bank, turn right along a riverside trail. This quickly follows a tributary upstream to cross via a footbridge and then heads back to the South Tyne.

Featherstone Castle, a private residence, consists of a Jacobean manor house and a pele tower dating from the 1330s. It was the ancestral home of the Featherstonehaugh family from the time of the Norman Conquest until the 18th century.

Reaching a road, turn right and then left through a gate – signposted Wydon. This clear track leads to the farm at **Wydon Eals**. As it nears the buildings, it bends right. At this point, strike off left to cross a stile a few metres to the left of a farm gate. Follow an overgrown path beside the fence on your right and then, after the next stile, head up to the left. Walk with the fence/wall on your right. About 15m after going through a gate, veer away from the fence to climb a faint trail through the trees. Cross a stile in the top fence and turn right to walk beside the fence on the right.

Once over the next stile, continue in roughly the same direction, aiming for a gate to the right of a hedgerow on the other side of the field. Beyond this, keep close to the fence on your left and then go through the next gate to join a clear track. This soon swings right and drops to **Wydon**. Follow the track between the farm buildings.

Having crossed a bridge over a tributary of the South Tyne, the track swings right. As it does so, cross the stile on the right – signposted Haltwhistle. Follow the path under the road bridge and, when you reach some allotments, turn right up the surfaced lane. At the next junction, turn right – signposted Bellister Castle. Having crossed back over the South Tyne, take the riverside path on the left. As you near the next bridge, bear right at a fork to reach a surfaced lane. Turn left. Immediately after the bridge, head up the path on the left to return to Haltwhistle Station.

Dropping towards Wydon near the end of the walk

WALK 32
Hadrian's Wall Path and Thirlwall Castle

Start/finish	Thirlwall View car park on B6318, 500m north of Greenhead (NY 658 659)
Distance	8.1km (5 miles)
Total ascent	169m (554ft)
Grade	1/2
Walking time	2½hr
Terrain	Riverside trail, farmland, quiet lane; short sections may be overgrown in summer; wet ground beside Pow Charney Burn
Maps	OS Explorer OL43; OS Landranger 86
Transport	Nearby Greenhead is served by buses AD122 (seasonal) and 185; Gilsland by the 185 only
Facilities	Ye Olde Forge tearoom and Greenhead Hotel in Greenhead; House of Meg tearoom, Bridge Inn and Samson Inn, all in Gilsland

This meandering walk takes in some of the lovely countryside on Northumberland's border with Cumbria. Among the many highlights are a section of the Hadrian's Wall Path, one of the best preserved Roman milecastles along the wall, the River Irthing and Thirlwall Castle's romantic ruins. The route briefly crosses the county boundary to call in at Gilsland at roughly the half-way mark, where two pubs and a café provide the opportunity for rest and refreshment.

From the car park, turn right and walk along the road for about 280m. Head up the steps on the left and cross the ladder stile to join the Hadrian's Wall Path – signposted Gilsland. Walking with a wall on your right at first, the way ahead across the farmland is fairly clear thanks in part to the white acorns on gateposts (the symbol of the National Trails). On reaching a rough track, turn right. When the track bends right, cross the stile to the left of it to continue on the National Trail. At the next lane, cross diagonally right and go through a kissing-gate. The route soon winds its way along the bottom edge of someone's front garden and then leaves via a ladder stile. Now head slightly left and walk along the bottom of a ditch. At the next gate, drop left on to a narrow lane. Go straight across and through a gate. After the next gate, turn right and descend towards the railway. Turn left, but don't follow the path heading to the right – under the railway. Instead, keep straight ahead through the gap – signposted Poltross Burn. The narrow path drops to cross the pretty, wooded ravine via a footbridge, entering Cumbria as it does so. After the steps on the other side, you'll see the remains of a Roman **Milecastle** on your left.

> The **Poltross Burn Milecastle** is one of the largest and best preserved on Hadrian's Wall. It contained two rows of barracks, the walls of which are still visible today.

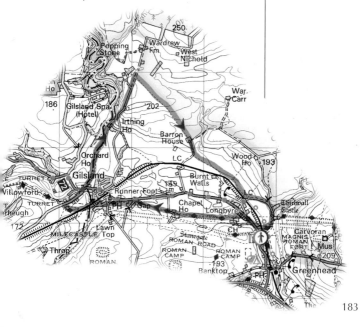

*Poltross Burn
Milecastle*

Beyond the milecastle, go through a kissing-gate and follow the narrow path beside the railway. Carefully checking for trains before you do so, cross the tracks at the next kissing-gate. The Hadrian's Wall Path drops left on the other side. After yet another kissing-gate, make your way towards a fence corner – ahead and slightly right. Follow the fence up to the road on the edge of **Gilsland**. Turn right and, parting company with the Hadrian's Wall Path, follow the road downhill. Turn right at the bottom – towards Greenhead. Immediately after passing the Northumberland county border sign, turn left – signposted Irthing House.

The rough track quickly becomes a lovely riverside trail. Sometimes the peat-laden River Irthing is on your immediate left; sometimes you have a fence between the path and the water. As you head upstream, you'll pass a set of steps down to the left. These lead to some stepping stones over the river – and back into Cumbria. Ignore them. After a wooden step stile, the path comes away from the river slightly as it nears **Irthing House**. Follow the track between the buildings but then, as soon as it bends right, go through the small gate opposite. A faint trail heads steeply uphill. On reaching a waymarker post close to a fence corner, bear right and cross a stile.

Turn left along the quiet lane. ▶

The large building on the opposite bank of the River Irthing is the **Gilsland Spa Hotel**, first built in the 1740s and rebuilt after a devastating fire in 1859.

Ignore the track to Wardrew House on the left, but then cross the stile on the right in another 175m – signposted Longbyre. A faint trail heads southeast through the long grass. As it then makes its way down to a ladder stile, you get a real sense of the height you've gained since leaving Gilsland. From this lonely spot, you can see the crags of the Great Whin Sill to the east, the Pennine moorlands to the south and the Lake District to the southwest. Beyond the ladder stile, the faint trail disappears. Continue in the same direction, making for the buildings at **Barron House**. After a large gate, follow the muddy track downhill. Go through the middle of the farmyard and then follow the access lane for 170m. As it bends right, cross the stile on the left.

There is no obvious path crossing the flat, damp ground immediately in front of you. Head southeast, passing about half-way between the two nearest power poles. As you progress across increasingly wet ground and through increasingly long grass, watch for wooden bridge railings ahead. Make your way to these. Cross the bridge and turn left to walk with the tiny Pow Charney Burn on your left. After a gate and bridge, the now clearer path swings right to reach a junction of trails. Turn left along a wet, but clear path. At the next waymarked junction, cross the ladder stile on the right. You're soon walking beside the railway.

On reaching a surfaced lane, turn left. Go right at the next junction and keep right past the farm buildings to follow a stony track downhill. As you near the next group of buildings, you'll see a small gate on the right. This is where you rejoin the Hadrian's Wall Path, but first,

As you climb, look behind to enjoy the views to the south: on a clear day you can see the northern Lake District, and Criffel beyond the Solway Firth.

Thirlwall Castle

you might want to explore the ruins of **Thirlwall Castle** up to the left.

The word '**Thirlwall**' comes from Old English, meaning 'gap in the wall', and probably refers to the break in Hadrian's Wall created by the Tipalt Burn. It was adopted by the local family who built the castle here, probably in the late 13th or early 14th century. Once a substantial stronghold against border raiders, its gradual decay began after the Thirlwalls moved to Hexham and then, in 1748, sold the castle to the Earl of Carlisle. Today, its walls are home to swifts and several species of bat.

Having rejoined the Hadrian's Wall Path, follow it across a cycle path and over the railway to reach the B6318. Turn left to return to the car park.

NORTH PENNINES

The view west from the Carriers' Way (Walk 35)

187

WALK 33

Allenmill Flues

Start/finish	Main square in Allendale Town (NY 837 558)
Distance	18.7km (11½ miles)
Total ascent	515m (1690ft)
Grade	2/3
Walking time	5½hr
Terrain	Quiet roads; good moorland tracks and paths; farm paths; woodland track; riverside path
Maps	OS Explorer OL43; OS Landranger 87
Transport	Bus 688
Facilities	Pubs, cafés and public toilets in Allendale Town

A walk of contrasts that starts by heading up on to the open moors above Allendale. Here, as well as grand views, are some of the most impressive remains of the area's once thriving lead industry. Two flues lead up on to the moors: These used to carry noxious fumes from the smelt mill way back down in the valley, almost 4kms away, to be released into the atmosphere via two chimneys that still stand tall on the moorland today. Beyond Dryburn Moor, farmland, rough pasture, woods and a long section of road walking eventually lead back to Allendale where the varied day ends with a lovely riverside path, particularly gorgeous in spring and autumn.

Take the road heading downhill beside the Allendale Forge Studio. The road crosses the River East Allen. Just as it bends right to head up the hill, take the lane on the left. Soon after the Friends' Meeting House, bear right at a fork. Turn left at a T-junction and then take the next road on the right.

Just after the farm at Frolar Meadows, turn left along a narrow lane. The remains of two flues can be seen now – one on either side of the road, with the one on the left leading directly to a prominent chimney on the moors ahead. After a cattle grid, keep to the stony track until it

Allendale's smelting mill flues lead up to these two vertical chimneys on the moorland

ALLENDALE MINES

During the 18th and 19th centuries, Allendale was the site of some of the most productive lead mines in the North Pennines. The main smelting mill occupied a sprawling riverside site just to the northwest of Allendale Town. Its first flue was built in 1808, but the main period of construction was the late 1830s. The mill's flue system condensed the poisonous fumes produced by the furnaces, carrying them for 4km up on to the open moorland and then releasing what was left into the air via vertical chimneys.

Deposits of valuable minerals would build up on the internal walls over time, and these would be removed at regular intervals. Entering via small doors in the flues, boys would be sent in to scrape the minerals, such as lead and even silver, from the stonework. Because of lead's toxicity, this must've been one of the deadliest jobs associated with the industry, apart from mining itself. Lead poisoning is associated with abdominal problems, learning difficulties in children, memory loss, kidney disease, high blood pressure, reproductive issues and problems relating to the central nervous system. It's even thought that the regular use of skin whitener containing lead contributed to the death of Queen Elizabeth I.

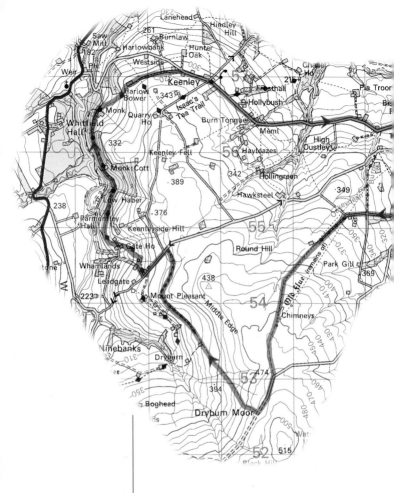

Gaps in the stonework allow you to peer into the tunnels, but don't climb on them: the stonework is unstable.

bends right at Fell House. Keep straight on here – along a grassier track rising beside the western flue. The track climbs sedately, and, on a clear day, you won't want to rush this section: the views across the dales and moors are superb. ◀ The track passes to the west of two **chimneys**, the first tall and slender, the second rather dumpier.

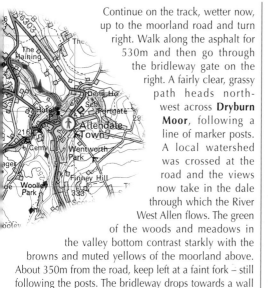

Continue on the track, wetter now, up to the moorland road and turn right. Walk along the asphalt for 530m and then go through the bridleway gate on the right. A fairly clear, grassy path heads north-west across **Dryburn Moor**, following a line of marker posts. A local watershed was crossed at the road and the views now take in the dale through which the River West Allen flows. The green of the woods and meadows in the valley bottom contrast starkly with the browns and muted yellows of the moorland above. About 350m from the road, keep left at a faint fork – still following the posts. The bridleway drops towards a wall and continues to the right of this. After a gate, the path is

Walking across Dryburn Moor

Looking across West Allen Dale from Dryburn Moor

briefly confined by walls on both sides. Shortly after leaving this walled section, keep right along the higher track, climbing slightly. This eventually leads to a minor road, along which you turn left.

Having walked along the asphalt for 450m, go through a small gate on the right – signposted Harlow Bower. You're now on Isaac's Tea Trail.

Isaac's Tea Trail is a 58km circular walk celebrating the life of a 19th-century itinerant tea-seller and philanthropist called Isaac Holden. Inspired by his conversion to Methodism, he also sold his own poems and early 'photographs' to help raise money for the Pennine villages' poor and needy.

Walk beside the fence on the right. Continue in the same direction after the next gate. Cross a ladder stile and drop left – through a gate to the right of a cottage. Head diagonally right across the next field, aiming for a gate to the right of a line of trees. Climb the short slope to the wind turbine and then drop gradually, aiming to the right of the buildings at **Gate House**. Go through a gate to drop on to a track. Turn right and, as soon as the track bends sharp right, go through the farm gate on the left. The way ahead isn't obvious, but walkers have beaten a trail through the thistles and nettles straight ahead. It descends, parallel with the wall on the left. Emerging from the prickles, continue beside the wall for a few more metres and then watch for a waymarker post ahead. This marks the point at which the path starts climbing a bracken-covered slope.

At the top, follow the wall on the right to a gate leading into Monk Wood. A track leads into the trees, becoming clearer as it progresses through a delightful mix of deciduous and coniferous species high above the River West Allen. **Monk Cottage** is passed after 800m. Another 800m of easy walking leads to The Monk Farm.

Immediately after the buildings, leave the track and veer right, keeping to the left of the sheds. Go through the farm gate on the left and walk to the fence on the left side of the field. Follow this uphill to a small gate. Once through this, look to the left and you'll see a line of poles carrying power lines up the field. Follow these to reach a small gate in the top wall. Cross diagonally left and follow the wall up to the buildings at **Harlow Bower**. Go through the metal gate and follow the farm track northeast. This is followed to a minor road – parting company with Isaac's Tea Trail along the way.

Turn right along the asphalt. There's a long stretch of road walking ahead – about 4.7km in total. It's 4km to the five-way junction at **Thornley Gate**. Turn left here – towards Catton and Hexham.

As the road drops towards the River East Allen, watch for the remains of the bottom end of the smelting flue in a garden to the right. Later, the site of the old smelting mill, now a commercial complex, is also passed.

Immediately after crossing the river, go through the gate on the right – signposted Allendale Town. This pleasant riverside path eventually comes out just above the road bridge crossed at the start of the walk. Turn left to reach the village. Turn left again at Allendale Forge Studio to return to the main square.

WALK 34

Above Allenheads

Start/finish	Parking area at Shorngate Cross on the minor road linking Allenheads with Rookhope (NY 871 450), on the left about 1.6km (1 mile) east of Allenheads on the Northumberland–County Durham border
Distance	21.4km (13¼ miles)
Total ascent	476m (1560ft)
Grade	3
Walking time	6hr
Terrain	Moorland tracks and paths; riverside trails; quiet lane; some damp sections
Maps	OS Explorer OL43 and OL31 (both required); OS Landranger 87
Transport	Bus 688
Facilities	Allenheads Inn, The Hemmel café and public toilets in Allenheads

This walk will appeal to those who love to stride out for easy miles under big, boundless skies with no one but the sheep and birds for company. But if you're not fond of track walking or grouse moorland, look away now... Starting from a high point of about 540m, this walk mostly uses shooters' tracks to enjoy the moorland above Allendale. Your only companions will be the sheep and the many birds that nest on the high ground, including curlew, golden plover, redshank and grouse. The return route uses a combination of gorgeous riverside paths and quiet lanes to reach Allenheads before the climb back to the parking area.

Walk northwest along the road for 300m and take the track rising to the right – signposted Byerhope Bank. After 2.6km of easy track walking in the **Byerhope** area, with good views down the valley, turn right at a junction marked by a tall cairn. The track passes just to the north of the trig pillar on **Green Hill** (529m) and continues to

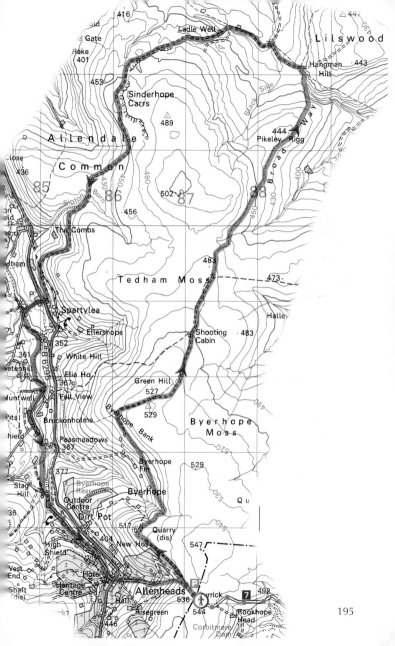

195

The Long Drag was built to carry lead from Allenheads to Hexham

a couple of shooting huts (**Shooting Cabin** on the OS maps). About 900m beyond these huts, you reach a fence.

Go through the gate here and, ignoring the clear track to the right, keep straight ahead (north-northeast) on a less-travelled route. At first, the path is broad and stony, but it becomes gentler underfoot as it passes around the eastern base of Harwood Carrs, a surprisingly rocky summit in an otherwise stone-free scene. The path passes through one gate and later swings left through a second one. It then drops to pass around the top of Rowantree Cleugh. ◄ Back on dry land, a stony path leads up to a crossing of ways. Turn left here, along another broad shooters' track. At the next track junction, close to some pipe lines, turn left again.

The ground is very wet here, requiring some agility as you leap from one grassy tuft to another.

> This track, followed for several kilometres, is known as the **Long Drag**. It was built to carry lead from the mines at Allenheads to Hexham.

Soon after another shooters' cabin, the track swings left. Ignore a track off to the left on the bend; simply keep to the route heading up the northern side of the cleugh. It quickly passes a small hut servicing the **Ladle Well** underground reservoir and later cuts beneath the exposed rocks of **Sinderhope Carrs**.

About 3.7km beyond the last shooters' cabin, the track crosses the substantial bridge over **Sipton Burn**. Soon after this, it begins its descent to the valley, passing through several wall gaps and crossing a couple of cattle grids along the way.

Just above the buildings of **Spartylea**, go through the gate on the right and follow the enclosed path down to the road. Go straight across to follow a minor road downhill. Immediately after crossing the River East Allen, take the footpath on the left – signposted B6295. This passes in front of a cottage and then crosses a stile. A narrow trail through the grass heads upstream, keeping close to the fence on the left. It crosses another stile and reaches a rough track. Go through the gate on the left to pass in front of the old corn mill and reach a bridge. Don't cross; instead go through the gate between the bridge and St Peter's Church to access a riverside path – signposted Peasmeadows and Dirt Pot.

Bridge over Sipton Burn

The route keeps close to the river. First, you're on a lovely path; then you pick up a track which becomes a surfaced lane. When the lane swings away from the river, take the signposted path on the left, staying close to the water's edge. After a picnic bench, the way ahead is less obvious as it crosses damp ground. Simply keep to the river bank across the access land, watching, in late spring, for the vibrant purple flowers of the mountain pansy, a lead-tolerant species that thrives on mine spoil.

Turn left at the road, over the bridge, and then right – signposted Allenheads and Ropehaugh. This quiet lane makes its way through **Allenheads** village, passing the pub, café and heritage centre. Just after the Gin Hill mine shaft, you reach the B6295. Cross straight over to follow a minor road uphill towards Rookhope, soon passing the pony track once used to access the mine.

During the 18th and 19th centuries, **Allenheads** was the site of the most productive lead mine in the North Pennines. Although the mine closed in 1896, this wasn't the end of the area's involvement in mining: in 1969, British Steel reopened the mine in search of fluorspar, used in the iron, steel and chemical industries. This subsequently closed in 1981.

You could follow this road all the way back to the parking area, about 1.6km from the B6295. Alternatively, to cut the corner, take the path signposted to Rookhope Road on the right as the road bends left. This quickly crosses a stile and then keeps to the left of a dank ditch. After a ladder stile, continue uphill beside the wall. Turn right on reaching a rough track and then right again at the road. The parking area is on the left in 90m.

WALK 35
Blanchland Moor

Start/finish	Large car park on northern edge of Blanchland (NY 964 504)
Distance	12.9km (8 miles)
Total ascent	259m (850ft)
Grade	2
Walking time	3½hr
Terrain	Quiet lane; good tracks, including forest; open moorland; farmland
Maps	OS Explorer OL43; OS Landranger 87
Transport	Bus 773
Facilities	White Monk Tearoom and Lord Crewe Arms, Blanchland

This is the first of two walks that explore the high ground above the pretty conservation village of Blanchland on Northumberland's border with County Durham. It heads north across Blanchland Moor at first – a land of big, dramatic skies. On a clear day, the views from here are breathtaking, and include the Cheviot Hills about 70km to the north. It is hard to believe, as you gaze into the distance, that the highest point on this track is less than 400m above sea level. After a brief flirtation with the edge of the sprawling Slaley Forest, the route returns via a wonderful bridleway on the western edge of the high ground. With little to worry about underfoot and not much in the way of ascent or descent, you can really stride out and enjoy the wide, open spaces.

From the car park, turn left along the quiet lane. After passing the cottages at **Shildon** and the remains of the old lead mine engine house, keep straight ahead on what is now a rough track.

As the track finally swings right to reach **Pennypie House** on the edge of the moors, go through the large gate on the left – signposted Ladycross and Burntshield Haugh.

The track across the heather moors provides good views north

BLANCHLAND

Blanchland was established in 1169 when a Premonstratensian abbey was founded here. The order began in northern France and was a sort of ecclesiastical middle ground for those who wanted something of the isolated life of prayer and discipline of the Cistercians and, at the same time, wished to serve their communities, like the Augustinians. The monks were known as the 'white canons' because their robes were made from undyed sheep fleeces – hence the village name, meaning 'white land'. Many of the beautiful buildings which exist in the conservation village today were built using the stones of the original abbey. These include the Lord Crewe Arms, which started life as the abbot's lodge and, in the 17th century, became the manor house.

The village was bought by the Bishop of Durham, Nathaniel Lord Crewe, in 1708. When he died in 1721, it became part of a charitable trust established by his will. To this day, Blanchland remains the centrepiece of the estate owned and conserved by that trust, the Lord Crewe Charity. The trust also has land and properties on the Northumberland coast at Seahouses, and makes grants to members of the clergy in the dioceses of Durham and Newcastle, largely to support their children's education.

Bear right and keep to the broad track rising gently beside the wall on the right. After going through a gate, you lose this wall; keep straight ahead on the clear track across the open moorland. This is a thoroughly enjoyable section of the walk with superb views ahead.

After going through a gate at a high point on the moor, ignore the track to the right. The route eases its way gently down-hill towards **Slaley Forest**. Nearing the thick wall of conifers, keep right at a fork – following the clearer track. This enters Forestry Commission land via a large gate.

Ignore a track on the right in a short while, but then take the next turning on the left. About 370m after passing another track off to the right, bear left at a fork.

Go through the gate in the forest fence and turn left, climbing gently beside the fence on your left. Reaching a gate, turn right along a narrow trail through the heather, keeping close to the fence on the left. This soon joins a bridleway from the right, which eventually passes through a gate.

You're now on the **Carriers' Way**, a packhorse route used in the 18th century to carry smelted lead to the River Tyne.

This is the point at which walks 35 and 36 meet: to combine the two to form a 19.5km circuit, keep straight ahead.

Although peaty, the bridleway is great to walk: the ground is relatively firm and its location on the edge of the high moorland means walkers have superb views across Devil's Water to the west. Go straight across one track close to a metal shooting hut. About 450m after a gate in a wall, bear left at a waymarked fork. ◄

The Carriers' Way, a packhorse route once used to transport smelted lead

This path on **Birkside Fell** isn't as clear as the others followed so far and there are some damp, peaty patches to cross, but waymarker posts guide the way. Beyond a gate, you're back on firm ground as the now obvious path makes its way gently downhill.

Reaching the point at which a wooden fence meets a wall, ignore the gate in the wall; instead, go through the gate in the fence. Now walk with the wall on your immediate right. At the far end of this narrow enclosure, go through the gate over to the left. Follow the wall round to the right and then drop to a rough lane. Follow this downhill to a sharp right-hand bend. Go through the gate on the left here – signposted Blanchland.

A clear grassy path leads across the top edge of the field, through a gap in the next fence and then continues in the same direction to pass through a small gate. The narrow path now keeps close to the fence on your right. The next gate leads on to a wide track, along which you turn right. Follow it between the buildings at **Cote House Farm**. It later swings left and drops to the lane followed at the start of the walk. Turn right to retrace your steps to the car park.

WALK 36

Birkside Fell and Beldon Burn

Start/finish	Large car park on northern edge of Blanchland (NY 964 504)
Distance	14km (8¾ miles)
Total ascent	324m (1063ft)
Grade	2/3
Walking time	3¾hr
Terrain	Good tracks; farm paths; open moorland; riverside path
Maps	OS Explorer OL43 and 307 (both required); OS Landranger 87
Transport	Bus 773
Facilities	White Monk Tearoom and Lord Crewe Arms, Blanchland

The second walk from Blanchland heads back up on to Birkside Fell to explore more of the lovely old packhorse route known as the Carriers' Way. Passing Bronze Age remains and a glacial meltwater channel along the way, it crosses moorland with a wonderful feeling of spaciousness. It almost seems a shame to leave the heather behind – but the walk still holds many delights. Following an excellent track through the striking valley occupied by Beldon Burn, it eases its way back towards Blanchland. Then, just when you think the route can't possibly have anything more to offer, there's one final surprise in store – a gorgeous riverside trail to end a perfect half-day.

From the car park, head left along the lane. After 130m, turn left along **Cote House Farm**'s access track. Ignoring a track signposted to the farm on the left, follow the main lane up between the buildings and then straight on between dry-stone walls. When the walled track ends, go through the gate on the left to follow a path along a fenced strip. After the next gate, continue in the same direction, along the top edge of two fields. Turn right when you reach a surfaced lane. Keep to this surfaced route when a rough track soon goes left.

The asphalt ends at a National Grid compound. Just a few strides short of the compound, bear right along a rough track. Follow this for about 70m and then, at a fingerpost, head left to locate a gate to the right of the walled compound. Once through this, the bridleway swings right – beside a wall. After a gate and stile, the grassy path swings right and then bends left, staying parallel with the wall for now. Before long though, they begin to part company. After the next gate, the way ahead is less clear – it heads generally northwest through the heather on **Birkside Fell**. Occasional waymarker posts lead the way.

On reaching a junction with another path, turn left. This is the **Carriers' Way**, the packhorse route followed in Walk 35. ▶ Just before passing under some power lines, watch for a Bronze Age ring cairn to the left.

When this **cairn** was excavated in 1997, the pit was found to contain a large urn, a flint knife and the cremated remains of two adults.

The valley of Beldon Burn

Walks 35 and 36 meet at this point, if you're thinking of combining them.

205

Evening sun on the woods and farmland west of Blanchland

Cross a stile next to a gate, pass to the immediate right of a shooting hut and then follow a fence gently uphill to a track junction. Turn right here and then, in 55m, turn left along a grassier track. The route becomes less obvious, but the general direction of travel is west-southwest.

Devil's Water flows through the sparsely populated valley to the right. It was near here, in AD634, that King Oswald's army finally killed the Celtic leader Cadwallon after the Battle of Heavenfield (see Walk 27). This paved the way for the spread of Christianity throughout Northumbria.

If you manage to stick to the right-of-way, you'll eventually find yourself

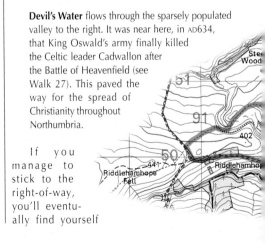

standing on the northeastern edge of a striking glacial meltwater channel. However, there's a chance you'll have been tempted by other, equally clear trails to stray slightly further south. In this case, you'll come to a fence and tumbledown wall marking the edge of a felled plantation. Turn right to walk beside the fence. At the corner of the plantation, keep straight on along the top of the slope that drops into the flat area occupied by the meltwater channel. Before long, as the path descends, you'll rejoin the right-of-way coming in from the right. The route now heads southwest through the bracken along the edge of the flat, damp ground.

Watch for a stile on the left. Cross this and the ensuing boardwalk. Pass to the right of a neat, round sheepfold. The path, obscured by bracken in the summer, heads diagonally up the slope to the right. At the top of the rise, cross an area devoid of vegetation to continue in roughly the same direction (west-southwest, veering southwest) on a narrow trail through the heather.

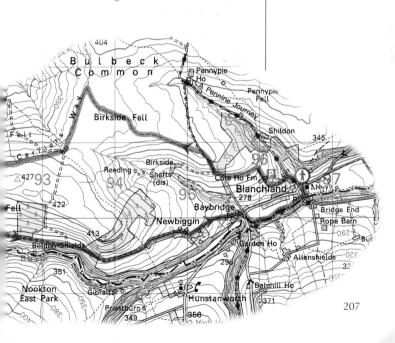

Cross a stile in a fence and turn left along a stony track. Keep left at a fork. After a gate, the track swings left to begin its return to Blanchland, parallel with **Beldon Burn** down to the right. The route passes to the left of the abandoned buildings at **Riddlehamhope**.

> The main building was used as a **shooting lodge** in the 19th century. To the west of it are the crumbling walls and rubble of a bastle.

At first, the track is a soft carpet of grass, but it later becomes stonier. Eventually, it passes the farm buildings at **Newbiggin** and bends left. Keep straight on along the surfaced lane, past Newbiggin Hall. At a road junction, turn right. Just before the road crosses Beldon Burn, take the path on the left – signposted Carrick and Blanchland. Before long, you're on a charming riverside path that skips in and out of the trees as it makes its way downstream.

On the edge of Blanchland, the path swings away from the river, crosses a tributary bridge and goes through a gap in a wall. Turn right and immediately left along the main road through the village.

Just after the Lord Crewe Arms, the road swings right. Just before it does so, take the road straight ahead. This passes to the left of the tearoom. The car park is on the left in a few metres.

APPENDIX A

Route summary table

No	Walk	Start/finish	Distance	Time	Page
Northeast Northumberland, including the coast					
1	Craster and Howick Hall	Craster Quarry car park, Craster (NU 256 197)	9.2km (5¾ miles)	2½hr	28
2	Dunstanburgh Castle and Low Newton	Craster Quarry pay-and-display car park, Craster (NU 256 197)	12.4km (7¾ miles)	3½hr	32
3	Seahouses to Belford	War Memorial roundabout, Seahouses (NU 219 320); market cross, Belford (NU 108 339)	17.2km (10¾ miles)	4¾hr	36
4	Lindisfarne	First pay-and-display car park on the island (NU 126 424)	8.9km (5½ miles)	2½hr	42
5	Berwick-upon-Tweed to Eyemouth	Parking area at Berwick Pier (NU 005 527); bus stop in Eyemouth (NT 944 644)	16.4km (10¼ miles)	5½hr	47
6	Norham Castle and River Tweed	Arched entrance to Norham Castle grounds (NT 906 475)	10.8km (6¾ miles)	3hr	54
7	St Cuthbert's Cave and the Kyloe Hills	Small car park at Holburn Grange (NU 050 350)	15.4km (9½ miles)	4¼hr	59
8	Doddington Moor	Junction of Wooler Golf Course lane and B6525 in Doddington (NT 999 324)	7.2km (4½ miles)	2hr	64
9	Bewick Moor	Forestry Commission car park at Hepburn Wood (NU 071 248)	15.3km (9½ miles)	4¾hr	68

No	Walk	Start/finish	Distance	Time	Page
National Park (north), including the Cheviot Hills					
10	Yeavering Bell from Wooler	Free car park at Padgepool Place, Burnhouse Road, Wooler (NT 989 281)	17.6km (11 miles)	5½hr	76
11	Great Hetha, the border and Ring Chesters	National Park car park at Hethpool, northern end of College Valley (NT 894 280)	12.8km (8 miles)	4½hr	82
12	The Cheviot	Roadside parking in Harthope Valley, near sheepfold beside Hawsen Burn (NT 953 225)	14km (8¾ miles)	5¼hr	87
13	Ancient Ingram	Small National Park car park at Ingram Bridge (NU 017 163)	10.1km (6¼ miles)	3¼hr	92
14	Breamish Valley and Salter's Road	Roadside parking at Hartside at the end of the public road through the Breamish Valley (NT 977 162)	17.6km (11 miles)	5hr	96
15	Harbottle	Forestry Commission's West Wood car park at Harbottle (NT 926 048)	6.5km (4 miles)	2¼hr	101
16	Wether Cairn	National Park car park, Alwinton (NT 919 063)	15.2km (9½ miles)	4¾hr	104
17	Clennell Street and Usway Burn	National Park car park, Alwinton (NT 919 063)	21.6km (13½ miles)	6¾hr	109
18	Border Ridge including Windy Gyle	Parking area at Buckham's Bridge, 15km northwest of Alwinton (NT 824 107)	18.5km (11½ miles)	5¾hr	114
19	Thrunton Wood	Main parking area at Thrunton Wood (NU 085 097)	13.4km (8¼ miles)	4¼hr	119
20	Rothbury Terraces	Cowhaugh car park beside River Coquet, Rothbury (NU 056 014)	9km (5½ miles)	3hr	123

No	Walk	Start/finish	Distance	Time	Page
21	The Simonside Hills	Forestry Commission's Simonside car park (NZ 037 997)	12.1km (7½ miles)	3¾hr	128
Kielder					
22	Tarsetdale Bastles	Parking area at Black Middens Bastle (NY 772 898), 11.6km northwest of Bellingham	13km (8 miles)	4hr	134
23	Bull Crag Peninsula	Large car park at Leaplish Waterside Park, Kielder Water (NY 660 877)	10.1km (6¼ miles)	3hr	139
24	Cat Cairn, Lewis Burn and Lakeside Way (south)	Car park at bottom of the track leading to Kielder Observatory (NY 626 928)	18.7km (11½ miles)	5½hr	142
25	Kielder Forest and Lakeside Way (north)	Pay-and-display car park at Kielder Castle (NY 632 937)	12.1km (7½ miles)	3¾hr	147
26	Deadwater Fell and Peel Fell	Pay-and-display car park at Kielder Castle (NY 632 937)	20.5km (12¾ miles)	6hr	152
Tyne Valley and National Park (south) including Hadrian's Wall					
27	Heavenfield and Wall	Roadside parking at Heavenfield on the B6318 (NY 936 694)	6.8km (4¼ miles)	2¼hr	158
28	Hadrian's Wall and Greenlee Lough	Steel Rigg car park near Once Brewed (NY 751 676)	12.2km (7½ miles)	3¾hr	162
29	Vindolanda and Crag Lough	Steel Rigg car park near Once Brewed (NY 751 676)	8.5km (5¼ miles)	2½hr	167
30	Best of Hadrian's Wall	Car park at Walltown Crags near Greenhead (NY 668 659); car park at Housesteads Fort (NY 792 683)	13.9km (8½ miles)	5hr	171

No	Walk	Start/finish	Distance	Time	Page
31	Haltwhistle and the South Tyne	Haltwhistle Railway Station (NY 704 637)	15.6km (9¾ miles)	4hr	176
32	Hadrian's Wall Path and Thirlwall Castle	Thirlwall View car park on B6318, 500m north of Greenhead (NY 658 659)	8.1km (5 miles)	2½hr	182
North Pennines					
33	Allenmill Flues	Main square in Allendale Town (NY 837 558)	18.7km (11½ miles)	5½hr	188
34	Above Allenheads	Shorngate Cross, on minor road linking Allenheads with Rookhope (NY 871 450)	21.4km (13¼ miles)	6hr	194
35	Blanchland Moor	Large car park on northern edge of Blanchland (NY 964 504)	12.9km (8 miles)	3½hr	199
36	Birkside Fell and Beldon Burn	Large car park on northern edge of Blanchland (NY 964 504)	14km (8¾ miles)	3¾hr	204

APPENDIX B
Useful contacts

Information centres

Wooler Tourist information Centre
The Cheviot Centre
Padgepool Place
Wooler
NE71 6BL
Tel: 01668 282123

Bellingham Tourist Information Centre
Station Yard
Woodburn Road
Bellingham
NE48 2DG
Tel: 01434 220616

Corbridge Tourist Information Centre
Hill Street
Corbridge
NE45 5AA
Tel: 01434 632815

Hexham Tourist Information Centre
Wentworth Car Park
Hexham
NE46 1QE
Tel: 01434 652220

Morpeth Tourist Information Centre
The Chantry
Bridge Street
Morpeth
NE61 1PJ
Tel: 01670 500700

Otterburn Mill
Tourist Information Centre
Otterburn
NE19 1JT
Tel: 01830 520093

The Sill National Landscape
Discovery Centre
Once Brewed
Near Bardon Mill
NE47 7AN
Tel: 01434 341200

The Information Kiosk
Walltown Quarry Country Park
Near Greenhead
CA8 7JD
Tel: 01434 344396

Other useful sources of information

Northumberland Tourism
www.visitnorthumberland.com

Northumberland National Park
www.northumberlandnationalpark.
org.uk

Northumberland Coast Area of
Outstanding Natural Beauty
www.northumberlandcoastaonb.org

North Pennines Area of Outstanding
Natural Beauty
www.northpennines.org.uk

Access restrictions
www.openaccess.naturalengland.org.uk

Traveline
0871 200 2233
www.traveline.info

Mountain Weather Information Service
www.mwis.org.uk

Meteorological Office
www.metoffice.gov.uk

NOTES

NOTES

NOTES

NOTES

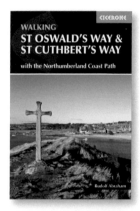
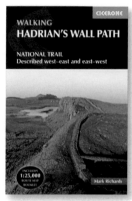

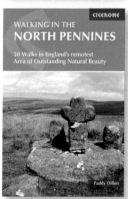

LISTING OF CICERONE GUIDES

SCOTLAND
Backpacker's Britain:
  Northern Scotland
Ben Nevis and Glen Coe
Cycling in the Hebrides
Great Mountain Days in Scotland
Mountain Biking in Southern and
  Central Scotland
Mountain Biking in West and
  North West Scotland
Not the West Highland Way
  Scotland
Scotland's Best Small Mountains
Scotland's Far West
Scotland's Mountain Ridges
Scrambles in Lochaber
The Ayrshire and Arran
  Coastal Paths
The Border Country
The Cape Wrath Trail
The Great Glen Way
The Great Glen Way Map Booklet
The Hebridean Way
The Hebrides
The Isle of Mull
The Isle of Skye
The Skye Trail
The Southern Upland Way
The Speyside Way
The Speyside Way Map Booklet
The West Highland Way
Walking Highland Perthshire
Walking in Scotland's Far North
Walking in the Angus Glens
Walking in the Cairngorms
Walking in the Ochils, Campsie
  Fells and Lomond Hills
Walking in the Pentland Hills
Walking in the Southern Uplands
Walking in Torridon
Walking Loch Lomond and
  the Trossachs
Walking on Arran
Walking on Harris and Lewis
Walking on Jura, Islay
  and Colonsay
Walking on Rum and the
  Small Isles
Walking on the Orkney and
  Shetland Isles
Walking on Uist and Barra
Walking the Corbetts Vol 1
Walking the Corbetts Vol 2
Walking the Galloway Hills
Walking the Munros Vol 1
Walking the Munros Vol 2
West Highland Way Map Booklet

Winter Climbs Ben Nevis and
  Glen Coe
Winter Climbs in the Cairngorms

NORTHERN ENGLAND TRAILS
Hadrian's Wall Path
Hadrian's Wall Path Map Booklet
Pennine Way Map Booklet
The Coast to Coast Walk
The Coast to Coast Map Booklet
The Dales Way
The Pennine Way

LAKE DISTRICT
Cycling in the Lake District
Great Mountain Days in the
  Lake District
Lake District Winter Climbs
Lake District:
  High Level and Fell Walks
Lake District:
  Low Level and Lake Walks
Lakeland Fellranger
Mountain Biking in the
  Lake District
Scafell Pike
Scrambles in the Lake District
  – North
Scrambles in the Lake District
  – South
Short Walks in Lakeland
  Book 1: South Lakeland
Short Walks in Lakeland
  Book 2: North Lakeland
Short Walks in Lakeland
  Book 3: West Lakeland
Tour of the Lake District
Trail and Fell Running in the
  Lake District

NORTH WEST ENGLAND
AND THE ISLE OF MAN
Cycling the Pennine Bridleway
Isle of Man Coastal Path
The Lancashire Cycleway
The Lune Valley and Howgills
The Ribble Way
Walking in Cumbria's Eden Valley
Walking in Lancashire
Walking in the Forest of Bowland
  and Pendle
Walking on the Isle of Man
Walking on the West
  Pennine Moors
Walks in Lancashire
  Witch Country
Walks in Ribble Country
Walks in Silverdale and Arnside

NORTH EAST ENGLAND,
YORKSHIRE DALES
AND PENNINES
Cycling in the Yorkshire Dales
Great Mountain Days in
  the Pennines
Historic Walks in North Yorkshire
Mountain Biking in the
  Yorkshire Dales
South Pennine Walks
St Oswald's Way and
  St Cuthbert's Way
The Cleveland Way and the
  Yorkshire Wolds Way
The Cleveland Way Map Booklet
The North York Moors
The Reivers Way
The Teesdale Way
Walking in County Durham
Walking in Northumberland
Walking in the North Pennines
Walking in the Yorkshire Dales:
  North and East
Walking in the Yorkshire Dales:
  South and West
Walks in Dales Country
Walks in the Yorkshire Dales

WALES AND WELSH BORDERS
Glyndwr's Way
Great Mountain Days
  in Snowdonia
Hillwalking in Shropshire
Hillwalking in Wales – Vol 1
Hillwalking in Wales – Vol 2
Mountain Walking in Snowdonia
Offa's Dyke Path
Offa's Dyke Map Booklet
Pembrokeshire Coast Path
  Map Booklet
Ridges of Snowdonia
Scrambles in Snowdonia
The Ascent of Snowdon
The Ceredigion and Snowdonia
  Coast Paths
The Pembrokeshire Coast Path
The Severn Way
The Snowdonia Way
The Wales Coast Path
The Wye Valley Walk
Walking in Carmarthenshire
Walking in Pembrokeshire
Walking in the Forest of Dean
Walking in the South
  Wales Valleys
Walking in the Wye Valley
Walking on the Brecon Beacons

For full information on all our
guides, books and eBooks,
visit our website:
www.cicerone.co.uk

Walking – Trekking – Mountaineering – Climbing – Cycling

Over 40 years, Cicerone have built up an outstanding collection of over 300 guides, inspiring all sorts of amazing adventures.

Every guide comes from extensive exploration and research by our expert authors, all with a passion for their subjects. They are frequently praised, endorsed and used by clubs, instructors and outdoor organisations.

All our titles can now be bought as **e-books**, **ePubs** and **Kindle** files and we also have an online magazine – **Cicerone Extra** – with features to help cyclists, climbers, walkers and trekkers choose their next adventure, at home or abroad.

Our website shows any **new information** we've had in since a book was published. Please do let us know if you find anything has changed, so that we can publish the latest details. On our **website** you'll also find great ideas and lots of detailed information about what's inside every guide and you can buy **individual routes** from many of them online.

It's easy to keep in touch with what's going on at Cicerone by getting our monthly **free e-newsletter**, which is full of offers, competitions, up-to-date information and topical articles. You can subscribe on our home page and also follow us on **Facebook** and **Twitter** or dip into our **blog**.

Cicerone – the very best guides for exploring the world.

CICERONE

Juniper House, Murley Moss, Oxenholme Road, Kendal, Cumbria LA9 7RL
Tel: 015395 62069 info@cicerone.co.uk
www.cicerone.co.uk